What happens when I pray?

and

Profiting from Prayer

What happens when I pray?

and

Profiting from Prayer

An abridgement and rewrite of the 'Theology of prayer' by B.M.Palmer (1818-1902), together with an abridged rewrite of 'The return of prayers' by Thomas Goodwin (1600-1680).

© Grace Publications Trust
139 Grosvenor Avenue
London N5 2NH
England

Joint Managing Editors
J.P.Arthur
H.J.Appleby

First published 1997

ISBN 0 946462 48 8

Distributed by
EVANGELICAL PRESS
Grange Close
Faverdale North
Darlington
DL3 0PH
England

Printed in Great Britain by:
Cox & Wyman Ltd., Reading

Cover design L.L.Evans

Part one

What happens when I pray?

Prepared by Dr N.R. Needham

Contents

Chapter   **Page**

Introduction

Benjamin Morgan Palmer (1818-1902) was one of the greatest and most famous Reformed preachers of America's Southern states in the 19th century. Sadly, most Christians today outside of the Southern states will not have heard of him. So what sort of man was he?

Palmer was born in South Carolina. This was the most proudly Southern of the Southern states, the first to declare its independence from the USA's federal government in the political crisis of 1860 which plunged America into civil war. However, Palmer's ancestors were actually Northerners — the Puritans of New England. Converted at the age of 18, Palmer trained for the Presbyterian ministry, and from 1843 to 1854 the young South Carolinian served as pastor of First Presbyterian Church of Columbia in his native state. He then acted for a few years as Professor of Church History and Polity at Columbia Seminary. Palmer's intellectual gifts meant that he could have become a great academic theologian; but the pastoral ministry was always his first love. So in 1856 Palmer returned to the pastorate, this time in the state of Louisiana, at First Presbyterian Church, New Orleans.

Palmer's ministry in Louisiana was interrupted in 1861-5 by the tragic devastation and bloodshed of the American Civil War (or as Southerners call it, the 'War between the States').

North and South fought each other; Northern forces captured New Orleans in May 1862, and Palmer took refuge in his native South Carolina. For those few years, he served as Professor of Theology at Columbia Seminary. When the War was over, and the South had been brutally crushed by the North, Palmer went back to First Presbyterian Church in New Orleans. There he helped Southern believers to rebuild their war-shattered lives. Palmer remained as pastor in New Orleans for the rest of his days.

Palmer has been called 'one of the greatest ministers of the Gospel the Southern Church has ever had'.[1] He gained a far-flung reputation in his own day as a powerful preacher, a compassionate counsellor and a wise church leader (and, incidentally, a distinguished friend and champion of the Jewish people). The high esteem in which Palmer was held is shown by the fact that in 1861, he was elected to be Moderator of the first General Assembly of the newly formed Southern Presbyterian Church. He wrote a number of valuable spiritual and doctrinal works, some of which have recently been reprinted.

This present Grace Publications book is based on Palmer's *Theology of Prayer*. This was written towards the end of Palmer's life in 1894. Palmer's biographer, T.C.Johnson, said of this book: 'It stands in a class by itself, and fills a gap which had existed hitherto in our theological literature.'[2] The book sets out to teach us both what prayer is and how we ought to pray, as well as dealing with some of the problems that can arise in our praying.

May God bless Benjamin Morgan Palmer's spiritual wisdom to a whole new generation of praying Christians today.

N.R.Needham   London 1997

[1]   M.H.Smith, *Studies in Presbyterian Theology*, p.218.
[2]   T.C.Johnson, *The Life and Letters of Benjamin Palmer*, p.573.

A note on this updated version of Palmer's 'Theology of Prayer'

I have drastically altered Palmer's style of writing to try to make it more accessible to modern readers. This has involved expanding some things Palmer says to bring out their meaning more fully. Palmer originally wrote in a highly condensed and poetic style, and any attempt at putting his thoughts into clear modern English must run some risk of paraphrasing rather freely. I believe I have been true to Palmer's meaning when I have done this. I have also rearranged quite a lot of the original. So if you are familiar with the *Theology of Prayer*, you might recognise passages in one place which you thought were in another. That is my doing, and again it was done to make Palmer's work easier to digest for modern readers. I have also added various Scripture quotations to illustrate some of the important points Palmer makes. All Scripture quotations are from the Revised Authorised Version.

At the end of all but the first chapter, I have included some 'points for reflection or discussion'. These are not in Palmer's original. They are intended to focus on some of the issues raised in each chapter, to help the reader think about them in a deeper way. They can also be used as a basis for discussion in a group which is working its way through the book.

NRN

1.
What are you doing when you pray?

'In this manner, therefore, pray: Our Father in heaven ...'
(Matthew 6:9). 'Ask, and it will be given to you; seek, and you
will find; knock, and it will be opened to you' (Matthew 7:7).
'Then he spoke a parable to this end, that men ought always to
pray and not lose heart' (Luke 19:1). 'Praying always with all
prayer and supplication in the Spirit' (Ephesians 6:18). 'Pray
without ceasing' (1 Thessalonians 5:17).

Clearly, God wants you to pray. The whole Bible makes
that obvious. But what exactly are you doing when you pray?

The spiritual activity of prayer is rather like the colours of
the spectrum. If you send a beam of white light through a glass
prism, the light spreads out into seven colours - red, orange,
yellow, green, blue, indigo and violet. In a similar way, if you
look closely at prayer you will find it spreading out into seven
'spiritual colours', or seven aspects of prayer. To these aspects
I am going to give the following names: adoration, praise,
petition, thanksgiving, confession, supplication and intercession.

I'm not saying that every single time you pray, you have to
make sure that your prayers are made up of all these seven
ingredients. I'm simply saying that prayer is a wide-ranging
activity which can include any of these 'spiritual colours'. You
need also to remember that like the seven colours of the

spectrum, these aspects of prayer blend easily into each other; you can't separate them too sharply. For example, adoration and praise blend together as worship.

Let's spend some time looking at these seven aspects of prayer.

2.
Adoration and praise

'Worship the Lord in the beauty of holiness' (Psalm 29:2).

Have you ever wondered why you exist? According to the Bible, the ultimate reason is to worship God. That's why God made you different from the animals, bestowing wonderful powers of thought and feeling on you. We human beings are designed to be the priests of creation; we give silent nature a voice with which to worship its great Creator.

All the powers of your soul equip you for this glorious purpose of worshipping your Creator. Your mind can think about him. Your heart can love him. Your longing for immortality makes you turn away from time to eternity. Then there is your conscience, that invisible judge within you, distinguishing between right and wrong. There is the instinctive reverence and awe that you feel for everything spiritual and divine. In fact, as a human being made in God's image, worship comes naturally to you, if only in the silence and solitude of your own thoughts.

But how can you worship God without praying? To bow down humbly in the dust before God's greatness — **that is the very essence of what prayer is**. It exists in your heart before it is expressed on your lips. It means recognising, in the inmost attitude of your spirit, the amazing contrast between the majestic Lord God almighty and your tiny self. To pray is to worship.

When we look at the worship expressed in the prayers of the Bible, we find it has two aspects, which I've called 'adoration' and 'praise'. Sometimes in the Bible we see people worshipping God for what he is in himself — his own glorious nature and being. This is what I call 'adoration'. Sometimes we see people worshipping God for what he does - his works, his mighty deeds in creating and ruling the universe. This is what I call 'praise'.

The difference between adoration and praise is very faint. They blend swiftly and naturally into each other. But there is a difference of emphasis, depending on whether we are looking more at who God is or what he does.

If you want to adore God in your prayers, to worship him for what he is in himself, how should you do it? You can learn from God's people in the Bible. They often expressed their adoration by means of the various names and titles of God. Here are a few examples of how they addressed God in their prayers:

The Lord God
The Lord our God
The Lord God Almighty
The great and awesome God
The great and mighty God
The Lord strong and mighty
The Lord of hosts
The Lord of lords
The King of kings
The King of glory
The Father of glory
The Most High
The High and Lofty One who inhabits eternity
The Maker of heaven and earth
The Lord our shield
The Lord our strength
The Lord our righteousness
The God of hope

The God of our salvation
The only wise God
The blessed and only Potentate
The King eternal, immortal, invisible
Our Father in heaven

You can see what a wonderful variety of ways the Biblical writers have of addressing God in prayer. Copy them! Adore God by giving back to him the names and titles he has given to himself in his Word. They will wake up your spiritual feelings and help you to speak to God in a worshipful way. They will also give you confidence to ask him to do things for you, by impressing on you how great and mighty his power, wisdom and love are.

God's people in the Bible also adored him by describing him in other ways in their prayers. Look at the following examples and see how they express deep spiritual adoration in the way they speak to God:

'Who is like you, O LORD, among the gods? Who is like you, glorious in holiness, fearful in praises, doing wonders?' (Exodus 15:11).

'Blessed are you, LORD God of Israel, our Father, for ever and ever. Yours, O LORD, is the greatness, the power and the glory, the victory and the majesty; for all that is in heaven and in earth is yours; yours is the kingdom, O LORD, and you are exalted as head over all' (1 Chronicles 29:10-11).

'He who is the blessed and only Potentate, the King of kings and Lord of lords, who alone has immortality, dwelling in unapproachable light, whom no man has seen or can see, to whom be honour and everlasting power. Amen' (1 Timothy 6:15-16).

'To God our Saviour, who alone is wise, be glory and majesty, dominion and power, both now and for ever. Amen' (Jude 25).

See how exalted these prayers of adoration are. They focus on God himself — who he is, what he is, his own brilliant nature and attributes, his greatness and majesty and holiness. This wonderful adoring worship teaches you an important lesson in your spiritual life: **you shouldn't limit your prayers to asking God to do things for you.** Is a feeling of need or a sense of guilt the only thing that will bring you to God? Will you come to God because you are empty, and then forget him when you are full? Don't be self-centred in your praying. God is infinitely beautiful in himself, and his beauty ought to attract you like a magnet to him. Can you think of a better use of your powers than to employ them in adoring your beautiful Lord? This aspect of prayer is independent of your changing moods and circumstances. Whatever state you may be in, God is always there, in the unchanging perfection of his supreme beauty and glory, to inspire your soul to worship.

Adoring God will have a healthy effect on your spiritual experience. When you adore him, you turn away from yourself and gaze on him in all his matchless loveliness and majesty. This will give new life to your spiritual feelings. It's so easy for Christians to get gloomy and despondent in their spiritual lives. Simply lying at God's feet, seeing him in his pure and lovely perfection, and adoring him for it, will help to drive away dark feelings; it will bring freshness and health back into your soul. It will help to cure you of your natural tendency to stare at yourself and be obsessed with your sins and problems. In fact, your whole spiritual life will suffer badly, unless you frequently adore the beautiful King of heaven in your prayers.

'But I can't always be adoring God.' That is true. There is something overwhelming and exhausting about concentrating the mind constantly on God himself. You will find your mind turning from God's infinitely glorious being to his works. Adoration passes over into praise. (Remember, worshipping God for his works is what I've called 'praise'). God's works reveal a little part of his glory at a time, and you will find that easier to bear than the pure and naked beauty of his being. You can dwell on a particular thing God has done, see how some aspect of his glory is revealed in it, and praise him for it.

If you want to see how God's people in the Bible praised him in their prayers for all that he had done, I suggest you read your way through the book of Psalms. Many of them pour out praise to God, both for his material and spiritual works:

'Sing praises to God, sing praises! Sing praises to our King, sing praises! For God is the King of all the earth; sing praises with understanding. God reigns over the nations; God sits on his holy throne' (Psalm 47:6-8).

'Praise the LORD! Oh give thanks to the LORD, for he is good! For his mercy endures for ever. Who can utter the mighty acts of the LORD? Or who can declare all his praise? ... Blessed be the LORD God of Israel from everlasting to everlasting! And let all the people say, "Amen!" Praise the Lord!' (Psalm 106:1-2, 48).

'Great is the LORD, and greatly to be praised; and his greatness is unsearchable. One generation shall praise your works to another, and shall declare your mighty acts. I will meditate on the glorious splendour of your majesty and on your wondrous works. People shall speak of the might of your awesome acts, and I will declare your greatness' (Psalm 145:3-6).

Your fellowship with God will never get closer to heaven than when you adore and praise him. The inhabitants of heaven are unceasingly adoring and praising their King. 'And they do not rest day or night, saying: "Holy, holy, holy, Lord God Almighty, who was and is and is to come!"' (Revelation 4:8). We, God's people on earth, should imitate our heavenly friends. The more you adore God for who he is, and the more you praise him for what he has done, the more of his spiritual radiance you will enjoy in your soul. You will be in tune with those who sing the new song in the Lord's presence (Revelation 5:9-10). What better way could there be of making yourself ready for heaven?

Points for reflection or discussion

What place should you give to adoration in your private and public prayers?

How much use do you make of God's various names and titles when you speak to him?

What does the Bible say about the 'beauty' of God?

'Sing praises with understanding' (Psalm 47:7; compare 1 Corinthians 14:15). What is the relationship between praise and understanding?

3.
Petition and thanksgiving

'I sought the LORD, and he heard me, and delivered me from all my fears' (Psalm 34:4).

When you pray, as well as worshipping God, you should also admit how much you depend on him. Now, being dependent on God is not something people like to acknowledge, especially not today with all the advances in science we are constantly making. People today are more likely to sing the praises of man than of God: glory to man in the highest, and glory to science! Our sense of dependence on God easily gets lost.

Ultimately, though, we have to come back to a simple and humbling fact. We did not create ourselves. God created us. As created beings, we are finite; our Creator-God is unlimited, but there are all kinds of limits to our lives from which we can't escape. Think about yourself for a moment. You can't stop yourself getting hungry or tired. Your knowledge, however great it may seem, is really very limited. If you are a Christian, even your spiritual life has its limits; you try to get close to God, but soon find yourself falling back exhausted to the created world. You have to admit it. 'How weak I am, how small, how ignorant!'

It's when you realise how needy you are that you discover another of prayer's 'spiritual colours' — what I call 'petition'. This simply means asking God to give you the blessings you need. Feeling how weak you are, you turn to God and ask him to give you some of his own boundless strength. Realising how little you know, you turn to God and ask him to share with you some of his perfect wisdom. Sensing your helplessness, and how incapable the world is of helping you, you say good-bye to yourself and the world; you turn to your merciful Creator, so that he can give you the help, comfort and peace you need, which only God can provide.

As an aspect of prayer, petition isn't something that applies to you only because you are sinful. Obviously you have needs that arise out of your sins, such as the need for forgiveness and new birth. But you have all sorts of other needs simply as a created being. Consider Adam and Eve before they sinned. They still depended on God for all the blessings that enriched their lives so wonderfully in paradise. They needed God to keep them alive, and to continue looking after them, providing them with food, drink and the blessedness of his own fellowship. I don't think it would have been wrong for them to express their sense of dependence on God by actually asking him to go on supplying their needs.

Petitionary prayer, then, applies to us as created beings, not just as sinners. I say this because there is a whole dimension of need and petition which does come out of our sinfulness, rather than out of our humanity. I want to look at this other dimension in the next chapter under the heading 'confession and supplication'. Here I'm emphasising the point that petitionary prayer, asking God for the blessings of life, is something absolutely basic to the relationship between us and our Creator. Dependence on God is your natural condition as a created being. You will never escape from it, not even when you finally escape from sin in heaven. So petition is a perfectly natural part of your relationship with God; it is part of being human. You become more truly human as you give up your proud independent spirit, and trust humbly in God through prayer to supply all your needs from the abundance of his divine resources.

22

The Bible is full of examples of petitionary prayer. The most famous is, of course, in the Lord's Prayer; 'Give us this day our daily bread' (Matthew 6:11). Here are some others:

'In my distress I called upon the LORD, and cried out to my God; he heard my voice from his temple, and my cry came before him, even to his ears' (Psalm 18:6).

'I am poor and needy; make haste to help me, O God! You are my help and my deliverer; O LORD, do not delay' (Psalm 70:5).

'Help us, O LORD our God, for we rest on you, and in your name we go against this multitude' (2 Chronicles 14:11).

'Give me neither poverty nor riches — feed me with the food you prescribe for me; lest I be full and deny you, and say, "Who is the LORD?" or lest I be poor and steal, and profane the name of my God' (Proverbs 30:8-9).

'O LORD of hosts, if you will give your maidservant a male child, then I will give him to the LORD all the days of his life, and no razor shall come near his head' (1 Samuel 1:11).

'Give to your servant an understanding heart to judge your people, that I may discern between good and evil' (1 Kings 3:9).

Here you see people asking God to bless them with comfort and help, relief from poverty and distress, strength in adversity, the right amount of food and money, the gift of a child, and moral and spiritual understanding. Be encouraged by their example. Carry all your needs to God in petitionary prayer. If you don't, you are claiming to be self-sufficient and independent of God — and that would be to live a lie.

If your sense of dependence on God makes you pray for blessings, it should also inspire you to thank him for blessings received. It's as if the sense of dependence gives birth to twins called 'petition' and 'thanksgiving': petition lifts up empty hands of prayer for God to fill, thanksgiving bows down with a prayer of gratitude for the gifts bestowed. At the heart of this twofold practice of petition and thanksgiving lies your recognition that God is the source of all true good, the fountain of all gifts and blessings. 'Every good gift and every perfect gift is from above, and comes down from the Father of lights, with whom there is no variation or shadow of turning' (James 1:17). That's why you pray to God to meet your needs. That's also why you should thank him when your needs are supplied out of his divine riches.

You can probably see that thanksgiving, like petition, is absolutely basic to your whole relationship with God as your Creator. If you acknowledge that relationship at all, you have to be thankful to God for every good thing you enjoy in your life. Lack of gratitude means you are trying to make out that you don't owe your blessings to God. That would be a total betrayal of your identity as someone he created and sustains. You would be basing your life on a massive falsehood. On the other hand, the more grateful you are to God for the good things you enjoy, the more you will be fulfilling your real identity as a created being; your life will be based on truth. So what I said about petition I can say again about its twin, thanksgiving: it is part of being human. The most thankful person is the most fully human person.

Here are a few examples of prayers of thanksgiving in the Bible:

'It is good to give thanks to the LORD, and to sing praises to your name, O Most High; to declare your lovingkindness in the morning, and your faithfulness every night' (Psalm 92:1-2).

'Oh give thanks to the LORD, for he is good! For his mercy endures for ever. Let the redeemed of the LORD say so, whom he has redeemed from the hand of the enemy ... Oh that men would give thanks to the LORD for his goodness, and for his wonderful works to the children of men! For he satisfies the longing soul, and fills the hungry with good things' (Psalm 107:1-2, 8-9).

'Then Jesus took the cup and gave thanks ... And he took the bread, gave thanks and broke it' (Luke 22:17, 19).

'We give thanks to God always for you all, making mention of you in our prayers' (1 Thessalonians 1:2).

'We give you thanks, O Lord God Almighty, the one who is and who was and who is to come, because you have taken your great power and reigned' (Revelation 11:17).

I said that these different aspects of prayer flow and blend into each other like the colours of the spectrum, and that we can't distinguish them too sharply. So you will notice how what I've called 'praise' and 'thanksgiving' can be different names for an expression of the same feeling. 'Enter into his gates with thanksgiving, and into his courts with praise' (Psalm 100:1). The psalmist didn't mean to distinguish sharply between thanksgiving and praise here.

However, I've used the two different words to try to point to a difference in emphasis. If you are worshipping God for his own beauty and glory, and you see these shining out of a particular thing that God has done, your main concern is with what that divine work shows you of God himself. It's slightly different if God does something that affects you personally, or affects your friends; your concern then will be the direct benefit of God's work to you or those you love. In both cases your response will be expressing your love to God for his wonderful work. But due to the different emphasis, I decided to call the first 'praise', because it is so close to adoration, and the second 'thanksgiving' because of its nearness to petition. As long as you realise there isn't any rigid distinction between them, you won't go wrong. It doesn't matter if you say you are 'thanking' God for a work that reveals his glory, or 'praising' him for a work that benefits you or your loved one. The important thing is actually to thank him and praise him in your prayers 'for his wonderful works to the children of men' (Psalm 107:8).

Points for reflection or discussion

'Dependence on God is your natural condition as a created being.' How dependent on God do you feel? Suggest ways in which the society you live in weakens or destroys your sense of dependence on God.

If you should ask God to supply your needs, how can you distinguish between what you need and what you want?

Find some other examples of petitionary prayer in the Bible. What do they teach you?

Discuss the sin of ingratitude. How can we become more thankful people?

4.
Confession and supplication

'If we say that we have no sin, we deceive ourselves and the truth is not in us. If we confess our sins, he is faithful and just to forgive us our sins and to cleanse us from all unrighteousness' (1 John 1:8-9).

The 'spiritual colours' of prayer we've looked at so far — adoration, praise, petition, thanksgiving — all belong to the basic relationship between intelligent beings and their Creator. It's part of your very identity as a man or woman created by God to pray in these ways. Adam and Eve before the fall would have prayed in these ways.

We now come to a new and darker 'spiritual colour' in the prayer spectrum. Confessing your sins to God and pleading for his mercy: these are not things that belong to the basic relationship between human beings and their Creator. Adam and Eve before the fall would not have prayed in this way. The entrance of sin into the world has added a new colour and tone to human praying. You need to pray now, not just as a created being to the one who made you and sustains you, but as a sinner to the one who judges you and can condemn or pardon you, destroy or save you.

Sin, disobeying God's holy law, makes you guilty in the sight of God. You may not **feel** guilty, but you **are**. It's an objective moral fact. As a guilty sinner, it is your duty to confess your sin to God. Confession basically means agreeing with God in his view of sin; you see it the way he sees it. It's often easy to see the distressing **consequences** of sin in people's lives, but you have to go further than that. You have to see how ugly and detestable sin is in itself, in its own dark nature. You have to view it in contrast to the beauty and purity of God's perfect character. Then you will see sin as he sees it, as something sick and repulsive beyond the power of words to describe.

When you see sin in this way, you will find yourself hating it. So don't be afraid of using strong language to express your feelings about sin. True confession brings with it a holy, burning horror and hatred of all sin, because sin is a vile thief, cheating God of his honour as well as robbing the sinner of his peace.

Following this holy resentment of sin, confession also involves passing judgement against it in your conscience. God condemns sin as a crime against himself that deserves the eternal death penalty. If you see it the way he does, you will echo this verdict in your own conscience. You will confess that God is righteous in judging and punishing sin so severely.

Finally, true confession includes repenting of your sin and abandoning it. I admit it may not be easy for you to break the habit of sin. Sadly, you may often find yourself tangled up again in the net you are trying to escape from. But at the moment when you actually confess your sin to God, it is your sincere wish to be free for ever from its bondage. If that isn't your honest desire, your confession is play-acting. You are deceiving yourself. You are even trying to deceive God.

You may have heard some Christians say that a justified believer shouldn't confess his guilt to God, because God has already washed it away in the blood of the Lord Jesus Christ. This is playing about with words. It is true that as a Christian, you are no longer guilty in the sense of being liable to punishment. However, you feel that you still deserve the punishment you have been saved from. That sense of what you deserve is what produces the need for confession. You agree with God that you deserve to be banished from his sight, even though he welcomes and accepts you for Christ's sake. If you didn't feel that you deserved God's righteous condemnation rather than his mercy, how could you have any true appreciation of his mercy?

Confessing your sins, then, is a vital aspect of your prayer-life. Here are some examples of God's people in the Bible confessing their sins to God:

'There is no soundness in my flesh because of your anger; nor is there any health in my bones because of my sin. For my iniquities have gone over my head; like a heavy burden they are too heavy for me. My wounds are foul and festering because of my foolishness' (Psalm 38:3-5).

'I acknowledge my transgressions, and my sin is ever before me. Against you, you only, have I sinned, and done this evil in your sight' (Psalm 51:3-4).

'Please let your ear be attentive and your eyes open, that you may hear the prayer of your servant which I pray before you now, day and night, for the children of Israel your servants, and confess the sins of the children of Israel which we have sinned against you. Both my father's house and I have sinned. We have acted very corruptly against you, and have not kept the commandments, the statutes, nor the ordinances which you commanded your servant Moses' (Nehemiah 1:6-7).

'I was speaking, praying and confessing my sin and the sin of my people Israel, and presenting my supplication before the LORD my God' (Daniel 9:20).

Follow the example of these godly people. Confess your sins to God. Your relationship with him will never be right if you don't. 'He who covers his sins will not prosper; but whoever confesses and forsakes them will have mercy' (Proverbs 28:13).

As I said when we looked at petition and thanksgiving, there is a whole new dimension of petition that you have to add to your prayers on account of your sins. You have to ask God to forgive you and also to set you free from sin's power. I've called this 'supplication', but it is really just petitionary prayer in relation to sin.

Obviously there is no point in confessing your sins unless you ask God to forgive them. In fact, praying for forgiveness is so important that the Lord Jesus Christ made it part of the model of daily prayer for his followers: 'Forgive us our debts, as we forgive our debtors' (Matthew 6:12). There are two points I want you to think about here. First, when you confess your sins and ask God's forgiveness, you aren't praying to someone who might say 'No.' In the gospel, God has promised to forgive all who draw near to him through the Lord Jesus Christ, confess their sins and request mercy. His answer is always 'Yes.' How can you possibly delay confessing your sin and seeking God's forgiveness if this is the case? 'Blessed is he whose transgression is forgiven, whose sin is covered ... I acknowledged my sin to you, and my iniquity I have not hidden. I said, "I will confess my transgressions to the LORD," and you forgave the iniquity of my sin' (Psalm 32:1,5).

The second point is that in the Lord's prayer, Christ teaches that you can't ask for God's forgiveness unless you are ready to forgive the people who have hurt you. God has joined these two things together; he wants confession and supplication to quench the fires of hatred and ill-will in the human heart. If you desire to receive God's forgiveness, you must have a forgiving spirit towards your neighbour. So when you approach God to confess to him the many sins you have committed, it should inspire you with compassion for the faults of others. 'Whenever you stand praying, if you have anything against anyone, forgive him, that your Father in heaven may also forgive your trespasses' (Mark 11:25).

As well as asking God to forgive you, you should also ask him to set you free from sin's power, to cleanse your heart of its polluting presence. This is what King David did after he had committed adultery with Bathsheba. He confessed his sin to God, asked for forgiveness, and also prayed that God would purify him inwardly: 'Create in me a clean heart, O God, and renew a steadfast spirit within me' (Psalm 51:10). Abandoning the sin you confess is essential to true confession, but you can't stop sinning without God's help. That's why supplication involves praying for sanctifying grace as well as forgiveness. 'Incline my heart to your testimonies, and not to covetousness. Turn my eyes away from looking at worthless things and revive me in your way' (Psalm 119:36-7).

Points for reflection or discussion

How can you get yourself and others to feel a true sense of guilt for sin? When is a sense of guilt false and unhealthy?

What sort of things might stop someone confessing his sins to God? What are the consequences of unconfessed sin?

How far should you confess your sins to other people?

Find some more Biblical examples of people praying for their own sanctification. Pick out and discuss two of them. You might find Psalm 119 a good place to start.

5.
Intercession

'Brethren, pray for us' (1 Thessalonians 5:25).

We come now to another dimension of petitionary prayer: praying for other people. This is so important that Christians usually give it the special name 'intercession', and that's what I've done too.

The Bible teaches in many places that we should pray, not just for our own needs, but for one another. The apostle Paul often prayed for others, and asked others to pray for him:

'Now I pray to God that you do no evil' (2 Corinthians 13:7).

'I do not cease to give thanks for you, making mention of you in my prayers, that the God of our Lord Jesus Christ, the Father of glory, may give to you the spirit of wisdom and revelation in the knowledge of him' (Ephesians 1:16).

'Now I beg you, brethren, through the Lord Jesus Christ, and through the love of the Spirit, that you strive together with me in your prayers to God for me' (Romans 15:30).

'Continue earnestly in prayer, being vigilant in it with thanksgiving, meanwhile praying also for us, that God would open to us a door for the word, to speak the mystery of Christ, for which I am in chains, that I may make it manifest, as I ought to speak' (Colossians 4:2-4).

Paul assured his friends that he was praying for them, and asked them in return to pray for him. As for actual examples of people interceding for others, we find prayers of this sort in both the Old and New Testaments. Look, for instance, at Abraham's prayer for Sodom in Genesis 18:23-32, Moses' prayer for Israel in Exodus 32:11-14 and Deuteronomy 9:25-9, and our Saviour's prayer for his people in John 17.

Intercession arises out of the fact that we humans are, by nature, social beings. 'For none of us lives to himself, and no-one dies to himself' (Romans 14:7). You can see this truth easily enough in your own life. Your very birth placed you in a network of human relationships through the family. These relationships multiply as you journey through life, meeting people and making friends. You can't opt out of the human race. If you tried, you would violate every instinct of your nature which tells you that you aren't a solitary isolated individual, but a member of mankind. In accordance with that truth, God wants you to come into his presence to pray as a member of the human race. Remember that next after loving him, God requires you to love your fellow men and women. What truer way of loving them could there be than lifting them up in the arms of prayer and carrying them to God? Prayer becomes an exercise of highest love when you forget about your own needs and sins, take up the cares and sorrows of other people, and lay them on the heart of God.

God has made each one of us his brother's keeper. In all our relationships, we are each other's guardians. That means that you are responsible for the influence you have on others. The apostle Paul was very concerned about the influence his behaviour might have on other Christians: 'Therefore if food makes my brother stumble, I will never again eat meat, lest I make my brother stumble' (1 Corinthians 8:13). The closer the relationship is, the more sacred is the trust God has given you. 'For how do you know, O wife, whether you will save your husband? Or how do you know O husband, whether you will save your wife' (1 Corinthians 7:16). But how can you really act as the guardian of your brothers and sisters, if you don't pray for them? There are all kinds of blessings that you don't actually have the power to give to anyone. You can only come to God and pray that he will give your neighbour those blessings. So don't be like Cain who denied that he had any responsibility for his brother. Accept your responsibility. Pray for your brother.

Intercessory prayer is part of the fellowship of believers in the great spiritual body of the church. You belong to your fellow Christians, and they belong to you. 'If one member suffers, all the members suffer with it; or if one member is honoured, all the members rejoice with it' (1 Corinthians 12:26). In intercessory praying, the church gathers together the various needs of all its members, and presents them lovingly to God. We meet with one another in the weakness we all share as created beings and guilty sinners, and together as one body we then pray to the God of all grace who can help us all.

Interceding for others will have a positive influence on your own soul. It will help to check the tendency you have (common to all Christians) to be self-centred even in your spiritual life. If you pray a lot for others, it helps you to forget yourself and makes you more sympathetic to your neighbour. King David gives us a great example of this unselfish spirit in Psalm 51. This is the prayer he prayed after his adultery with Bathsheba. He can't pour out his own guilt and shame to God without adding a prayer for God's people: 'Do good in your good pleasure to Zion; build the walls of Jerusalem. Then you shall be pleased with the sacrifices of righteousness, with burnt offerings and whole burnt offerings; then they shall offer bulls on your altar' (verses 18-19). Ask God to make you like David: an intercessor, even in the midst of your own great sins and great needs.

Points for reflection or discussion

Read through one of the examples of intercessory prayer mentioned in this chapter — Abraham praying for Sodom, Moses praying for Israel, the Lord Jesus Christ praying for his church. What can you learn from it?

The apostle Paul asked others to pray for him. When do you or should you do the same?

We often pray for one another's physical needs. How can we make sure we pray intelligently for each other's spiritual needs?

In what ways can we improve the intercessory aspect of our prayers, both as individuals and as a church?

6.
The spiritual benefits of praying

'Behold, he is praying!' (Acts 9:11)

If you build the habit of prayer into your life, it will have the most profound spiritual effect on you. In fact, prayer is one of God's chief ways of educating you spiritually. It's in the school of prayer that your soul will really develop, expand and reach its highest enjoyment.

Think about it this way. There are deep longings in your heart which created things can never satisfy. These longings point you to God your Creator as the only one who can bring you real satisfaction and fulfilment. But there is such a distance between your soul and God! How can you get to him? In his overflowing goodness, God has provided a bridge across which you can journey to him. That bridge is prayer. By travelling across this bridge to God, your deepest longings will be satisfied.

For instance, you have a natural curiosity, a thirst for knowledge; you want to understand why you exist, the meaning of life and how you should live. Only God can quench that deep thirst. He is the source of all knowledge, all light and wisdom. The only way you can get satisfaction for your mind is to go to God across the bridge of prayer, and enter into fellowship with him, the supreme mind, the fountain of wisdom and truth. 'No one knows the things of God except the Spirit of God. Now we have received, not the spirit of the world, but the Spirit who is from God, that we might know the things that have been freely given to us by God.' (1 Corinthians 2:11-12).

Or take the fact that you were created to love. Your heart can find real joy only through love — through loving and being loved. But look around you: there is nothing in this world of tiny, finite, created objects that can really satisfy your capacity for love. There is a good reason for that. God intends you to find that satisfaction in himself alone, by loving him, the infinitely loving and lovable Creator. Only God is big enough to satisfy your heart's capacity to give and receive love. So your heart has to go to him across the bridge of prayer, and enter into blessed union with him. 'I am my beloved's and my beloved is mine' (Song of Solomon 6:3).

You also have a deep hunger for beauty. You encounter it in the things around you. Throughout history, people have tried to reproduce or create beauty in sculpture, painting, music, poetry and prose. At the end of the day, though, these human works of art, and even the natural beauties of creation, can't satisfy you. You find yourself asking, 'Where is the original and ultimate beauty, the source of beauty, of which all these earthly things are just a dim shadowy reflection?' The answer is — God. The shadowy reflections of earthly beauty point upward to the beauty of the Creator himself. Only he can satisfy your hunger. You have to turn your face towards his by going to him across the bridge of prayer. 'One thing I have desired of the LORD, that will I seek: that I may dwell in the house of the LORD all the days of my life, to behold the beauty of the LORD' (Psalm 27:4).

See, then, how God educates your soul through prayer, nurturing your desires for truth, love and beauty, and teaching you to discover them in himself. Play truant from the school of prayer and you will never learn these things. You will be a spiritual ignoramus, shallow and undeveloped and unable to understand the things of the Spirit.

If you think carefully about this school of prayer, you will understand how praying strengthens every power God has given your soul, and blends them all together into a wonderful harmony. Prayer brings your human nature to perfection. (This is quite different to worldly people's ideas of a perfect man or woman; how many of their heroes pray?) For example, you can't really pray without thinking about what you're doing. In the words of the psalmist, 'I thought about my ways and turned my feet to your testimonies' (Psalm 119:59). 'I thought': there's a whole world of meaning in that little phrase. Before you can speak a single word of prayer, you have to think. You have to use your mind. You need to know who you're praying to. You need to know what you're praying for. You need to know the basis on which you are offering these prayers. So if your prayers are real, and not just some ritual of thoughtless words, they will involve you in a vigorous use of your understanding. As you come to pray, you will examine yourself, your motives, your past behaviour, your future destiny. You will search into all that you can possibly know of that glorious and beautiful Lord into whose presence your praying brings you. When you actually speak with him, you will spend all the riches of your intelligence in thoughtfully adoring, praising, petitioning and thanking him.

It isn't just your understanding but your conscience too that wakes up to life in prayer. In fact, it's in prayer more than anywhere else that conscience asserts its kingly rights. As you enter into God's holy presence through prayer, your conscience brings you face to face with your moral responsibilities; it keeps and displays a record of how faithful you've been in carrying out those responsibilities; it fastens on you the righteous sense of blame or approval. A healthy and active conscience depends on a healthy and active prayer-life. A dead or dying conscience is a terrifying symptom that prayer is dead or dying in your soul.

Praying also gives life to your heart, your spiritual emotions. As you pray, your spiritual vision will grow clearer. You will see that goodness isn't only your duty, but beautiful and desirable too; and sin isn't only wrong, but totally repulsive.

True prayer makes the heart recoil with horror from all evil and rush forward with eager desire to embrace the good.

So you can see how praying strengthens and perfects your human nature by setting your intelligence, conscience and feelings to work, and harmonising them all around God. The perfect man or woman is the one who has been made perfect through prayer. Ignore prayer, and you not only abandon God, you destroy yourself as a human being.

I've called prayer a 'bridge' across which you can journey to God. All the spiritual benefits of praying that I've just outlined depend on your actually making that journey and meeting God. Fellowship with him is the bright glory of prayer. Think of it; you, a finite and sinful created being, having personal prayer-communion with your infinite and holy Creator! As the proverb puts it, 'A man is known by the company he keeps.' Solomon says. 'He who walks with the wise shall be wise' (Proverbs 13:20). What shall we say, then, about a person who enjoys daily fellowship with the King of kings? Prayer can't be a trivial affair if it involves fellowship between your soul and the holy Sovereign of the universe.

Your fellowship with God through prayer has a number of glorious features. First, it's intensely personal. Each believer's communion with the Lord is deeply individual and intimate, a one-to-one relationship between God and his child. This is clearly true in private prayer. 'But you, when you pray, go into your room, and when you have shut your door, pray to your Father who is in the secret place' (Matthew 6:6). (That is 'you' singular in the Greek). This individual aspect of prayer is also true when you join together with other Christians to pray as a group or as a church. Each believer still experiences his own personal contact with God. The wonder of praying with other Christians is that each individual note of prayer blends in with all the others to create a sort of symphony of worship. But where would the symphony be without the individual notes?

Your fellowship with God in prayer is one of total trust. There is no shyness or reticence in prayer. Sins you wouldn't admit to your closest human friend you freely confess to your all-pardoning God. If you are going though some unhappiness that is too great for you to put into words, you can simply let yourself collapse in the Father's arms, and weep there. He will hold you. Even more wonderfully, God isn't shy or reticent when you really pray. He gives himself to you without any reservations. 'The secret of the LORD is with those who fear him, and he will show them his covenant' (Psalm 25:14). What peace he pours into your heart when he assures you of his forgiveness! What joy he sometimes gives you, when like Moses you go up 'into the thick darkness where God is' (Exodus 20:21)! It's part of the splendour of prayer that you and God give yourself to each other totally.

Your prayer-fellowship with God also puts you in touch with all his divine attributes. Whatever your need is, you will find something in God to match and meet it. Are you confused and ignorant? You can draw on the treasures of his perfect wisdom. Are you weak, broken and exhausted? You can receive from the supplies of his boundless strength. Are you impure and corrupt? You can open yourself to the rivers of his health-giving purity. Is your heart wounded, bleeding and fainting with sorrow? You can drink from the fathomless well of his supreme joy. You can continually fill the emptiness of your spirit from the eternal fountain of God's nature — the fountain from which you will drink for ever in paradise. All that God is will supply all that you need.

Your fellowship with God in prayer will also give you a proper view of time and eternity. When you cross the bridge of prayer, two worlds meet: the seen and the unseen. Prayer lifts your soul out of the crumbling ruins of time into the presence of 'the King eternal, immortal, invisible' (1 Timothy 1:17). The limits of time and space fall away, and you enter heaven and eternity, 'tasting the powers of the age to come' (Hebrews 6:5). Because prayer brings you face to face with the eternal God like this, it forces you to realise that the world you can see is under the control of a higher world you can't see. As a result, you begin to order your life in the light of that higher world. In this way prayer-communion with God helps to liberate you from being pathetically enslaved to the physical world of your senses; it builds up the supremacy of the spiritual over the physical. If you don't pray, you will never have a true appreciation of the relationship between earth and heaven, time and eternity. A prayerless person is like a prisoner locked up in the narrow darkness of the present. But the praying believer is like an eagle soaring through the sky in the light of the eternal sun.

You can see, then, what infinite unsearchable riches will come pouring into your soul from fellowship with God through prayer. Can you possibly hold yourself back from praying? But I haven't finished yet. There are still other spiritual benefits you will enjoy from a regular practice of prayer. For a start, have you ever thought about the effect it will have on your daily sanctification? If you want to 'put off the old man which grows corrupt according to its deceitful lusts, and be renewed in the spirit of your mind, and put on the new man which was created according to God in righteousness and true holiness' (Ephesians 4:22-4), you must be constant in prayer. Praying will nourish, deepen and strengthen the holy principles of the renewed mind God has given you in Christ. As you come into God's presence through prayer, your mind encounters him in all his perfection. You bow down with a sense of awe before his majestic greatness. You feel a mingled fear and trust as you look at his uncompromising justice. Affection and gratitude melt your heart as you see his grace and compassion. By bringing God before you in this way, prayer sanctifies your thought-processes into worship; it transforms your whole way of thinking. If you pray regularly, these inward acts of worship will become lasting habits, and the spiritual side of your nature will get ever greater mastery over fleshly appetites.

Regular prayer will strengthen you in your struggles with sin. All true obedience to God springs out of a heart that loves him. All disobedience springs ultimately out of a selfish heart that has broken away from him. By praying, if it's real prayer, you strike at the very roots of that selfishness. Prayer brings you into God's presence and humbles your proud heart in the dust before his overwhelming majesty, holiness and sovereignty. You say to him: 'Hallowed be your name, your kingdom come, your will be done' (Matthew 6:9). That means you have to let go of your sinful obsession with your own name, your own little kingdom and your own will. Through praying you break down your natural self-centredness, by acknowledging needs which God alone can satisfy, confessing sins which God alone can pardon, and giving thanks for blessings which God alone has provided. Prayer leads your rebel heart back into its proper subjection to God, making you less centred on yourself and more on him.

Praying will also make you spiritually fit for the practical tasks of life. This is true even when your prayers don't actually touch on your earthly duties and circumstances. Simply worshipping God and enjoying him in prayer will send you back into life's conflicts with renewed strength and freshness. This is even more clearly the case when your prayers arise out of the necessities of your life in this present world. If you ask for wisdom and guidance, that deepens your sense of obligation to follow God's will when you discern it. If you admit to God how weak you feel, that very admission stops you wasting in wrong activities what little strength you do have. If you ask God to help you in some specific situation, that very prayer will nurture patience and courage to do God's will in that situation. In these ways and many others, prayer will have a powerful secret influence on your character and life.

Regular habits of prayer will also lift your spiritual experience above the control of changing moods, and make it steadier and more balanced. Our moods can often mislead us about the true state of our souls. Young Christians in particular are likely to think that feeling happy is a sure sign of a healthy soul, and feeling gloomy a sure sign of a diseased one. But that isn't true. Your moods are affected by all kinds of non-spiritual factors.

For instance, your natural temperament will colour all your emotions. The physical condition of your body, in health and sickness, will have a big effect on the way your soul feels. Your outward circumstances, whether you are prosperous and successful or defeated and afflicted, will naturally uplift or depress you. Your emotional state also has an inner rhythm of its own, a natural sequence of ups and downs.

All this means that you have to be very careful in using your feelings as a guide to your spiritual state. You need to distinguish carefully between truly spiritual emotions, which are the fine bloom of Christian character, and other feelings which flow from non-spiritual factors.

It's precisely here that regular habits of prayer can help you. Prayer will give a clearness and a spiritual tone to your mind, as you leave earth behind you and enter into fellowship with God. This helps you to believe and trust God on the firm basis of his Word, even when everything around you is dark. Praying also nourishes your faith, hope and patience, so that they become strong and enduring habits of your mind. You can then take refuge in God from all the confusion of your changing moods and circumstances. The regular practice of prayer lifts your soul up above the shifting emotional shadows caused by non-spiritual factors, and helps to make your Christian experience calmer, more peaceful and more balanced.

Points for reflection or discussion

If prayer is as central to the Christian life as this chapter says, do you think there is enough teaching on it in the church? How central is prayer to the life of your own soul and your own church?

'Praying strengthens and perfects your human nature.' How far does the practice of prayer figure in your idea of the perfect man or woman? What about society's ideas, seen in films, TV shows and novels?

Pick out and discuss two of the ways this chapter says that prayer will contribute to your sanctification.

7.
God's blessings and petitionary prayer

'And so it was, when Moses held up his hand, that Israel prevailed; and when he let down his hand, Amalek prevailed' *(Exodus 17:11).*

So far I've spoken about the influence that prayer has on **us**. What about the influence it has on **God**? Can we speak about our prayers 'influencing' him? After all, we often ask God to do things for us in petitionary prayer, and we expect something to happen apart from the spiritual effect our praying has had on our own souls. There wouldn't be much point praying, 'Give us this day our daily bread' if the prayer only had a spiritual influence on our souls!

We need to think very clearly and carefully here. Despite the well-known phrase 'the power of prayer', prayer doesn't in fact have any power of its own. It isn't a kind of magic spell by which we can untie God's hands and enable him to act. It is better to think of it like this: when God decides to bestow some gift on us, that is a free, sovereign decision on his part; but he also prompts and inspires us to pray, so that our praying becomes the doorway through which his gift comes to us. As someone once put it, 'When God loosens your tongue with a request, it is because he wants to give you something.'

You can see this principle at work in what the apostle Paul says about petitionary prayer in Romans 8:26-7. 'Likewise the

Spirit also helps us in our weaknesses. For we do not know what we should pray for as we ought, but the Spirit makes intercession for us with groanings that cannot be uttered. Now he who searches the hearts knows what the mind of the Spirit is, because he makes intercession for the saints according to the will of God.' Paul tells us here that the Holy Spirit is the secret power behind our praying, and that he intercedes 'according to the will of God'. In his eternal wisdom and sovereignty, God the Father has already decided what gifts and blessings he wants to impart. God the Holy Spirit, whose will is one with the will of the Father, forms in the believer's heart a corresponding desire for those gifts and blessings. The believer prays for them. So the Father 'who searches the hearts' sees his own purpose of blessing reflected in the believer's prayer. The Holy Spirit has created a spiritual harmony between the believer's will and the Father's. This harmony is the channel God delights to use in blessing us.

Some Christians think that God's sovereignty takes away any meaning from our prayers, except the effect our praying has on ourselves. If (they say) God has already decided what blessings he is going to bestow, all our prayers can do is bring us into a receptive state of mind and make us ready to receive those blessings. Now while it is true that our prayers do bring us into a receptive state of mind, I think they do more than that. If all we are really doing in our prayers is just preparing ourselves, why address the prayers to God? Think about it. If you are talking to God merely to influence yourself, your prayers become unreal. You may as well stop praying **to** God and simply meditate **about** God. But genuine prayer is a real pleading with God. You focus your mind on him as the giver, not on yourself as the receiver.

So it isn't adequate to say that prayer just makes us ready to receive God's blessings. It is more than that. Prayer expresses a real personal relationship between you and God. God has given you intelligence, feelings, conscience and will. He wants you to use all these abilities fully in your relationship with him. That's why he has told you to practise prayer as the gateway through which he wants his blessings to come to you. He wants to involve you personally with himself in the way he blesses you. He does this through the gift of prayer, as you talk to him, express your needs to him, plead with him, and place your will in his will. The result is that you 'work out your own salvation with fear and trembling', while at the same time 'it is God who works in you to will and to work on behalf of his good pleasure' (Philippians 2:12-13). Your will and God's will, your work and God's work, mysteriously unite in prayer.

In fact, it's the same with your prayers as with the rest of your life. The sovereign Lord of the universe controls everything, but his control doesn't mean he tramples on your mind, feelings, conscience or will. He sovereignly works in them, with them and through them. Think about a farmer who ploughs the soil, sows the seed and cultivates a crop. Someone comes along and says to him, 'Why are you bothering to do this? Have you never heard of God's sovereignty? God has perfect wisdom and knows how to make this crop grow without your interference. God is perfectly good, so he will make the crop grow anyway, since he always does what is good. And God is in control, so the crop would have grown whatever you did, because God's purposes are eternal and unchangeable. Why don't you just go home and let God get on with it?'

This kind of argument would leave us all lying paralysed on our backs in case we insulted God's sovereignty by doing something. But this is not the way that God controls his world. His work doesn't abolish yours. He works in your work, with your work, and through your work. It's the same with prayer. God is the 'inspirer and hearer of prayer'. He works **in**, **with** and **through** your praying. In this way, he gives full scope for the activity of your own mind, feelings, conscience and will in the securing of his blessings. If he just gave you everything without making you ask, you would be more like an unreasoning animal than a person. By making you ask, God raises you up to the high dignity of being a person in a personal relationship with himself.

You shouldn't think, then, that God's sovereignty removes any meaning from your petitionary prayers except the effect they have on you. Your prayers are themselves part of God's sovereignty; he himself prompts and inspires your praying as the doorway for his gifts to come to you, so that he can honour your personhood in the way he blesses you. So petitionary prayer does have a sanctifying influence on you, but beyond even that, it also expresses the personal relationship between God and yourself which is the glory of being a Christian.

Points for reflection or discussion

In what ways can we treat prayer as if it were a magic spell?

How can a false understanding of God's sovereignty spoil our spiritual lives, especially our praying?

How would it change our relationship with God if he gave us everything without prayer?

8.
Prayer and God the Father

'When you pray, say: "Our Father in heaven ..."' (Luke 11:2)

When you are praying, you shouldn't think of God simply as 'Lord' or 'Creator', but as the Trinity. In the outworking of God's great purposes of salvation, recorded in the Bible, God has revealed that his divine nature doesn't exist in just one person but in three: the Father, the Son and the Holy Spirit. 'Go therefore and make disciples of all nations, baptizing them in the name of the Father and of the Son and of the Holy Spirit' (Matthew 28:19). The Trinity means that we worship one God in three persons. This sacred truth has vast implications for prayer.

For a start, you can pray to each of the three persons of the Trinity, because each one of them is completely and truly God. They aren't three gods, but one God: one divine being or nature eternally existing as three persons. The deep oneness of being which these three divine persons enjoy means that they can never be separated from each other; so you shouldn't separate them in your worship either, but worship all three equally as the one adorable God.

On top of this, each person of the Trinity plays a special individual role in your salvation. As a saved person, you have a threefold redemptive relationship with the Father, with the Son and with the Holy Spirit. You can pray to each divine person in all that concerns his particular part in your salvation.

For example, you can pray to the Father, praising him for adopting you as his beloved child. You can pray to the Son, thanking him for dying for you, since it was Christ, not the Father or the Holy Spirit, who took flesh and gave himself for you. You can pray to the Holy Spirit too as the one who indwells your heart and sanctifies you.

What we're going to look at over the next few chapters is the relationship between prayer and the different roles played by the three persons of the Trinity in our salvation. We begin by considering prayer and God the Father.

The first thing we need to realise here is this: God the Father is the official representative of all three divine persons in their joint-dealings with us. He acts on behalf of the whole Trinity, so that in our relationship with him as our Father we are actually relating to the Son and the Spirit too. This role of representative belongs naturally to the Father because he is the **first** person of the Trinity. It's possible that some of my readers may not be sure what it means to call the Father the 'first' person of the Trinity, so let me try to explain.

Among the three persons of the Trinity, quite apart from their dealings with us, there is an eternal order. The Father comes first in that order, because he is the origin or source of the other two persons. Beyond all limits and conceptions of time, God the Father eternally gives birth to his Son and eternally breathes forth his Holy Spirit. So within the life of the Trinity, the Son and the Spirit derive from the Father, like streams of water eternally flowing from a timeless fountain. But the Father himself derives from no-one. In that sense, God the Father is the first person of the Trinity. He isn't more 'God' than the Son or the Spirit, for they share fully the Father's divine nature; but he is their source.

The Father, then, occupies this first place in the eternal order within the life of the Trinity. So it's only fitting that he should also have first place in the order in which the three persons act towards us. That's why the Bible presents the

Father to us as the ultimate source of our salvation. He sent the Son into the world; the Son didn't send the Father. He gave the Holy Spirit to the Son in the river Jordan; the Son didn't give the Spirit to the Father. The Son offered himself on the cross to the Father, not the Father to the Son. And so on. Everything leads us back to the Father.

So I hope you can see how natural and appropriate it is for the Father, not the Son or the Spirit, to occupy the position of representative — the one who deals with us on behalf of all three divine persons. That's why the Father is often simply called 'God' in the Bible. It isn't that the Son and the Spirit are not God, but that the Father represents all three. And that's why the natural and normal way for you to pray is to speak to God the Father as the official representative of the Trinity in its wholeness and oneness. As the apostle Paul puts it, you go **to** the Father **through** the Son **by** the Spirit (Ephesians 2:18). Or as the Lord Jesus Christ taught in the 'model prayer', 'When you pray, say: "Our Father in heaven"' (Luke 11:2). This doesn't mean that you will never pray to the Son or to the Holy Spirit, but such prayers will be the exception rather than the rule. Generally you will pray to the Father.

Let me suggest another reason why you should normally address your prayers to God the Father. He is the person of the Trinity who upholds the claims of the divine law. I'm sure you already know that the plan of salvation needs a substitute to satisfy the claims of God's law on behalf of sinners — to obey its precepts and suffer its penalties for us. But if sinners need a representative, so does the law. Someone to uphold the law on God's behalf is just as necessary as someone to submit to the law on humanity's behalf.

The Bible shows us that the first and second persons of the Trinity carry out these corresponding roles. The Father acts as heavenly ruler and judge, maintaining the majestic authority of the law; the Son acts as humanity's substitute, submitting to the holy claims of the law. As the law's upholder, the Father accepts his Son's atoning work on our behalf, and declares it a righteous basis for saving sinners. 'God set Jesus forth to be a propitiation by his blood, through faith, to demonstrate his righteousness ... that he might be just and the justifier of the one who has faith in Jesus' (Romans 3:25-6). This means that God the Father is the one who officially justifies us from our sins and grants us all the blessings of salvation. 'If God is for us, who can be against us? He who did not spare his own Son, but delivered him up for us all, how shall he not with him also freely give us all things? Who shall bring a charge against God's elect? It is God who justifies. Who is he who condemns?' (Romans 8:31-4). ('God' here is clearly God the Father). So you should pray to the Father as the one who holds the administration of the law in his hands. It's the Father who has the authority to grant the pardon and life which his Son's obedience unto death has purchased for sinners.

Another reason why you should pray to the Father is that he is the one who adopts you into his family and makes you his beloved child. Of all the words we Christians use to describe our salvation, 'adoption' is probably the one that gives us the biggest and richest view of what God has done for us. Other descriptions of salvation are like the petals of a flower, which we peel away one by one; when we reach the flower's very heart and centre, we find adoption there.

Consider the glory of adoption! It points you to the wonderful change in your legal status, by which you cross over from being a mere slave to a precious child of God, with the right of access to your Father and the guarantee of a heavenly inheritance. 'For you did not receive the spirit of bondage again to fear, but you received the spirit of adoption by whom we cry "Abba, Father." The Spirit himself bears witness with our spirit that we are children of God, and if children, then heirs — heirs of God and joint heirs with Christ' (Romans 8:15-17). It also points you to the spiritual transformation by which God liberates you inwardly from sin's power and makes you his spiritual offspring, sharing in his holy nature — in other words, the new birth and sanctification. 'Behold what manner of love the Father has bestowed on us, that we should be called children of God! ... Whoever has been born of God does not sin, for his seed remains in him; and he cannot sin, because he has been born of God' (1 John 3:1,9). Adoption also points you forward to your glorification in the new heaven and the new earth, where you receive your full inheritance as God's child, see your Father face to face and enjoy him perfectly for ever. 'Creation itself also will be delivered from the bondage of corruption into the glorious liberty of the children of God. For we know that the whole creation groans and labours with birth pangs together until now. And we ourselves also, who have the first-fruits of the Spirit, groan within ourselves, eagerly waiting for the adoption, the redemption of our bodies' (Romans 8:21-3). In truth, adoption is a treasure chest overflowing with all the gems of salvation.

Adoption is the supremely glorious blessing; and the Father is the person of the Trinity who adopts you. He changes your legal status from a slave and an outcast to a beloved child, and bestows on you all the blessings and privileges which this new relationship involves. So here is another strong reason to address your prayers to the Father. The soul that is struggling in the agonies of new birth will cry out to the Father from whom this birth comes. The heart that is striving to throw off the spirit of bondage will plead with the Father to bestow the Spirit of adoption. And the believer who is enjoying the glorious freedom of being God's child will pour out his thanksgiving to the Father whose everlasting arms are sheltering him.

The final reason I want to suggest for why you should pray to the Father is that he is the supreme focus for Christian worship. We've already seen how important worship is as an aspect of prayer. We've also seen how the Bible reveals God as Father, Son and Holy Spirit, one God in three persons; you have to worship all three, because they are the one God. But we've also seen how the Father is the first person of the Trinity. He is eternally the origin of the Son and the Spirit, causing them to exist as his eternal co-equals who share his very nature. In that sense, the Father is the source of the unity within the Trinity. So the unity of God shines out specifically in the person of the Father. Also, remember that the Father officially represents all three divine persons in their joint-dealings with us. So the unity of all the Trinity's works and activities also shines out in the Father.

From all this, it follows that you ought to focus your worship of the Trinity on the person of the Father. Please don't misunderstand me. It isn't that you should worship him to the exclusion of the Lord Jesus Christ and the Holy Spirit. Of course not. What I mean is this: when you worship the whole Trinity as the one God, without distinguishing the persons, then you should direct your worship specifically to the Father. This is because he embodies the unity of the Trinity: both in the eternal life of the three persons among themselves, and in their dealings with us. In this sense, you should make the Father the supreme focus for your worship. In the words of the Son: 'The hour is coming, and is now, when the true worshippers will worship the Father in Spirit and truth; for the Father is seeking such to worship him' (John 4:23).

54

Points for reflection or discussion

How Father-centred are you in your spiritual life and worship? Do you think we sing enough hymns to God the Father?

What is wrong with praying normally and regularly to Jesus rather than to the Father?

Does adoption give us 'the biggest and richest view of what God has done for us'? If so, what place should it have in our thinking and preaching?

Suggest ways in which the Bible portrays the Father as the 'first' person of the Trinity and 'the ultimate source of our salvation'.

9.

Prayer and Christ as our Prophet

'Lord, teach us to pray' (Luke 11:1).

We come now to look at prayer in relation to God the Son. We aren't going to think about praying **to** the Lord Jesus Christ, since I've considered that already in the last chapter. What we're going to do here is look at how prayer relates to the three offices Christ assumed in the work of salvation - the offices of prophet, priest and king. We'll take them in that order, and begin with prayer in relation to Christ's office of prophet.

God promised Moses, 'I will raise up a Prophet like you from among their brethren, and will put my words in his mouth, and he shall speak to them all that I command him' (Deuteronomy 18:18). The New Testament makes it clear that this prophet is the Lord Jesus Christ (Acts 3:22-6). Christ, then, is your prophet. As such, he reveals God to you. Other prophets in the Old Testament had revealed something of God's will, but Christ reveals God perfectly. 'God, who at various times and in different ways spoke in time past to the fathers by the prophets, has in these last days spoken to us by his Son' (Hebrews 1:1-2).

Now, no created being can reveal the heart of God. Only Christ can do this, because he shares to the full the Father's divine nature. 'In the beginning was the Word, and the Word was with God, and the Word was God ... No-one has seen God at any time. The only-begotten Son, who is in the bosom of the Father, he has declared him' (John 1:1,18).

You may perhaps ask, 'But doesn't the Bible say there is a revelation of God in creation? Doesn't creation reveal the Creator?' Yes, that is true. Passages like Psalm 19:1-3 and Romans 1:19-20 teach this. But even creation is the Lord Jesus Christ's work. Prior to his incarnation, he, God the Son, made the universe by his mighty power. 'All things were made through him; and without him nothing was made that was made' (John 1:3). 'For by him all things were created that are in heaven and that are on earth, visible and invisible, whether thrones or dominions or principalities or powers. All things were created through him and for him' (Colossians 1:16). So creation itself is part of Christ's activity of revealing God to you.

However, creation only gives you a distant revelation of God. Your heart yearns for a more intimate, more personal communion with its Creator. This is especially true in view of your sinfulness. Your guilt-burdened heart cries out for God to show you his mercy and pardon, which creation can never reveal to you.

To quench the thirst of your heart, God the Son became man, assuming the office of a prophet. 'The Word became flesh and dwelt among us, and we beheld his glory, the glory as of the only-begotten of the Father, full of grace and truth' (John 1:14). As your prophet, the Lord Jesus Christ has unveiled God perfectly to you. 'I and *my* Father are one' (John 10:30). 'He who has seen me has seen the Father' (John 14:9). Here is a revelation of God exactly suited to your needs and longings as a sinful human being. Because you are human, the Son manifested the divine nature to you by becoming a human. The Lord Jesus Christ is, so to speak, God with a human face. How sweet and attractive this revelation is: the very heart of God opened up to you in a human soul and life. You can find and know God in the humanity of Jesus far more intimately than you ever could in stars, trees or flowers. And in Jesus you find God revealed to you, not just as your Creator, but as your compassionate Redeemer, bringing the free gift of salvation to you and your fallen race. Here is the mercy your sinful heart craves, which no amount of meditating on stars, trees or flowers could ever give you.

Jesus' revelation of the Father is what enables you truly to pray. 'We do not know,' Paul says, 'what we should pray for as we ought' (Romans 8:26). How can we, unless someone teaches us? We stumble about, groping in the dark, until we hear the voice of Christ our prophet saying to us: 'No one comes to the Father except through me' (John 14:6). Christ is the one who makes known to you the infinite riches of the Father's love, and the way of salvation along which God leads guilty sinners to paradise. This overwhelming revelation of God's redeeming grace and power is what inspires you with the boldness, hope and perseverance of true prayer. 'Through Christ we have access by the Spirit to the Father' (Ephesians 2:18). The person who knows Christ best is the person who will pray best.

Points for reflection or discussion

If creation cannot reveal God's saving mercy in Christ, should we sing 'Jesus is Lord! Creation's voice proclaims it'? As God the Son, Christ created the universe, but can we really learn from the stars, trees and flowers that 'Jesus is Lord'?

As our prophet, Jesus teaches us by example as well as by discourse. What can you learn about prayer from the example of Jesus' own prayer-life?

What are the benefits of the Son's revelation of God in human form? What do you see that wouldn't be clear from creation?

10.
Prayer and Christ as our Priest

'Therefore, brethren, having boldness to enter the Holy Place by the blood of Jesus, by a new and living way which he consecrated for us through the veil, that is, his flesh, and having a high priest over the house of God, let us draw near with a true heart in full assurance of faith' (Hebrews 10:19-22).

The Bible says that the Lord Jesus Christ is the priest of his believing people. What does that means for our prayers?

To answer that, we need to think about what our Saviour's priesthood really means. It involves two things. First, Jesus offered up his body and soul for us on the altar of the cross as a perfect sacrifice, to atone once and for all time for all our sins. 'Every priest stands ministering daily and offering repeatedly the same sacrifices, which can never take away sins. But this man, after he had offered one sacrifice for sins for ever, sat down at the right hand of God' (Hebrews 10:11-12). Second, having risen from the dead, Jesus now intercedes for us in heaven to secure our personal enjoyment of the blessings his death purchased for us. 'Because he continues for ever, he has an unchangeable priesthood. Therefore he is also able to save to the uttermost those who come to God through him, since he ever lives to make intercession for them' (Hebrews 7:24-5). These two aspects of Jesus' priestly work have a very close relationship with our praying.

In the first place, then, Jesus' atoning death on the cross is what gives you your wonderful freedom of approach to God. If you came before the King of the universe as an unforgiven sinner, the only thing you could expect from him would be righteous condemnation. How could you possibly pray in those circumstances? Your sense of God's rejection of you would choke the voice of prayer in the most hellish despair. But, Christian soul, you have a priest: Jesus' atoning sacrifice washes away all your guilt. Through the shedding of his blood, you have a full and free pardon for ever for all your sins. God no longer condemns you. 'There is therefore now no condemnation for those who are in Christ Jesus' (Romans 8:1). Surely this opens your heart and your lips into the freedom of prayer. You may now come into God's awesome presence, not as a condemned criminal, but as a forgiven, reconciled, accepted son or daughter!

So when you feel the attacks of a guilty conscience, accusing you fiercely of your sins, and your tormented soul cries out for peace with God, you know what to do. You must cling by faith to the priestly self-sacrifice of Jesus. Between your sin and God's holy anger, you place the death of his Son. Through that all-sufficient atoning sacrifice of your glorious priest, you can pray now with the joyful confidence that God accepts you, God hears you, and God grants you peace with himself. 'Therefore having been justified by faith, we have peace with God through our Lord Jesus Christ, through whom also we have access by faith into this grace in which we stand' (Romans 5:1-2).

Then, in the second place, your praying is also closely related to the priestly intercession which Jesus is now carrying out in heaven for his people. Your priest didn't only sacrifice himself for you. He also rose from the dead for you, ascended into heaven for you, and is now actively interceding for you in the holy presence of his Father. How he intercedes for you and for all his believing people, you can see from his priestly prayer in John 17: 'I pray for them. I do not pray for the world, but for those whom you have given me, for they are yours ... Holy Father, keep through your name those whom you have given me, that they may be one as we are ... I do not pray that you should take them out of the world, but that you should keep them from the evil one ... Sanctify them by your truth. Your word is truth ... I do not pray for these alone, but also for those who will believe in me through their word, that they all may be one, as you, Father, are in me and I in you; that they also may be one in us, that the world may believe that you sent me' (John 17:9,11,15,17,20-21).

The fact that your priest is both God and man in one person equips him perfectly for this great work of interceding for you. As God the Son, Christ knows everything. So he knows all about you, and knows exactly how to pray for you. As man, the experiences of suffering he went through in his earthly life give a deep and vital human sympathy to his prayers for you, as you go through various problems and trials. His human feelings reach out to all for whom he suffered, strengthening his desire to bring them all into the riches of blessing he purchased for them at the price of his own blood.

So in heaven, the glorified Lord Jesus Christ is praying for you right now. This truth should have a big impact on your own praying. In common with all Christians, you can sometimes be distracted in your prayers, because you feel so many doubts and fears rising out of your sense of weakness and unworthiness. How, you ask yourself, can God listen to such feeble prayers from such an unworthy sinner? What you need to realise is this: you are never alone when you pray. You never come to God by yourself. You come in union with the Lord Jesus Christ, your heavenly priest, who is himself praying for you. The only way you can pray is by mingling your prayers with those of Jesus and God the Father always listens to the prayers of his beloved Son.

This gives you the peaceful conviction that God will regard with favour your feeble praying. Your prayers don't come to him on their own, but blended with the beautiful and perfect praying of Jesus, whom God has appointed as your perfect priest. We could put it like this: God is not about to reject Jesus on account of those sin-stained prayers of yours which Jesus brings to him. On the contrary, God will gladly accept you and your sin-stained prayers on account of the sinless and beloved Jesus through whom you pray. So never let your sense of sin and unworthiness stop you from coming to God in prayer. You aren't alone. The Father has given you a great and compassionate high priest in Jesus. Jesus' sinless perfection and atoning sacrifice will sanctify your sinfully imperfect prayers, and make them into a sweet and fragrant spiritual incense, acceptable to God.

There is one last point I want to put to you. If you understand Jesus' heavenly priesthood, it will help you to see what makes your prayers effective. The key to all effective prayer is the harmony that exists between your own spiritual desires and the prayers your priest is offering in heaven. Those holy desires of your soul which you express in prayer haven't come from yourself. They come from the Holy Spirit. And the Spirit has taken these holy desires out of the heart of Jesus your priest, and placed them in your heart. By doing this, the Spirit creates a mysterious unity between you as you pray and your heavenly intercessor. You become one with Jesus; his powerful heavenly pleading flows down into your heart and becomes your praying. In other words, your praying on earth is really the Holy Spirit enabling you to echo Jesus' praying in heaven. You are sharing in the heavenly prayer-life of Jesus himself! Doesn't that make you realise what a glorious, beautiful and holy thing prayer is?

Points for reflection or discussion

How does the doctrine of Jesus' priesthood help you to pray?

Look at Jesus' 'high priestly prayer' in John 17. What is Jesus praying for in heaven for his people? How can we cooperate?

Think about how Jesus' two natures, human and divine, make him a perfect priest.

11.
Prayer and Christ as our King

'Blessing and honour and glory and power be to him who sits on the throne, and to the Lamb, for ever and ever!' (Revelation 5:13)

As well as being our prophet and priest, the Lord Jesus Christ is also his people's king, the royal son of David who reigns over an everlasting kingdom. 'He will be great, and will be called the Son of the Highest; and the Lord God will give him the throne of his father David. And he will reign over the house of Jacob for ever, and of his kingdom there will be no end' (Luke 1:32-3). As king, Christ actually applies to his people the blessings he purchased for us by his redeeming work on earth. Your sanctification in particular is a manifestation of Christ's kingship. Your king imparts his own glorious risen life to you, conquers your sins, makes you holy, protects you from falling back into Satan's power, and at last in the resurrection perfects you for the eternal life of heaven. He does all this by his Holy Spirit. 'Being exalted to the right hand of God, and having received from the Father the promise of the Holy Spirit, he poured out this which you now see and hear. For David did not ascend into the heavens, but he himself says: "The Lord said to my Lord. 'Sit at my right hand, till I make your enemies your footstool'"' (Acts 2:33-5). The Holy Spirit is the Spirit of the king Messiah.

When you pray, you are in contact with Christ the king. You ought to keep before your mind the wonderful truth that your whole spiritual life is in kingly hands. As you struggle with sin and temptation, and pray for grace, fix your eyes on your risen and exalted sovereign. He has royal power to answer those prayers and strengthen you with mighty grace. Remember that this king is your brother. You won't find an alien or a stranger sitting on the throne of the universe, but a fellow human being, one of us, a redeemer who is our kinsman. Our heavenly king can 'sympathise with our weaknesses', because he himself 'was tempted in all points as we are, yet without sin' (Hebrews 4:15). The practical conclusion for our praying which the writer of Hebrews draws from our exalted sovereign's humanity is: 'Let us therefore come boldly to the throne of grace, that we may obtain mercy and find grace to help in time of need' (Hebrews 4:16). You can come to this glorious king with warm confidence, because he is your sympathetic human brother.

Christ the king isn't just in control of your spiritual life. He is the sovereign Lord of all your circumstances. It is vital for a healthy prayer-life to grasp this truth. Together with all God's children, you will often find your experiences in life dark and depressing. The apostle Paul speaks about 'tribulation, distress, persecution, famine, nakedness, peril and sword' as the kind of things that can take hold of you and try to destroy your faith (Romans 8:35). If you see these things as falling on you from the will of a cold, distant, unsympathetic God, they will crush you and strangle the voice of prayer.

But how different everything will look if you fasten your eyes on Jesus your priest-king, and see him seated in beauty on the throne of the universe! The one who died for you is now ordering your circumstances by the self-same love he displayed for you on the cross. Surely you can trust him? If you have placed your faith in him for your final destiny in the life to come, you can also trust your loving Lord in all the affairs of this present life. By his royal power, he can make sure that 'all things work together for good to those who love God, to those who are called according to his purpose' (Romans 8:28).

So nothing can separate you from his love. He gave his very life's blood to redeem you, and he won't let any combination of circumstances destroy you. He is the king. He is in control. He is ready to pour out royal grace to help you in every harsh experience.

Believe this, and you will be able to pray prayers of unconquered faith in the midst of burning fire and drowning water.

Points for reflection or discussion

What does Christ's kingship mean for your attitude to your everyday life and spiritual struggles?

'Let us come boldly to the throne of grace' (Hebrews 4:15). What gives us boldness to come?

Compare Christ's kingship and priesthood. What points of similarity and difference can you see? How does each encourage you to pray?

12.
Prayer and the Holy Spirit

'Praying always with all prayer and supplication in the Spirit'
(Ephesians 6:18).

The official title Scripture gives to the Holy Spirit in the work of salvation is 'the Helper'[1] (John 14:16, 26; 15:26; 16:7). This comes from the Greek word **paracletos**, which has been turned into an English word as 'paraclete.' Interestingly, Scripture also gives the Lord Jesus Christ this title in 1 John 2:1: 'If any man sins, we have an Advocate with the Father, Jesus Christ the righteous.' The word 'Advocate' here is the same Greek word **paracletos**. Christ spoke about both himself and the Holy Spirit as paracletes at the same time in John 14:16. So what does this word mean?

A paraclete is someone who comes and stands alongside you to help you when you are in trouble. For instance, if you got involved in legal difficulties, you would hire a lawyer and he would plead your case for you in court. The lawyer would be your paraclete. Or if you were seriously ill, you would call in a doctor to find out what was wrong with you and bring you back to health. The doctor would be your paraclete.

In your eternal salvation, you have two paracletes: the Lord Jesus Christ and the Holy Spirit. Christ is like a lawyer, dealing

---

[1] 'Helper' is the way the Revised Authorised Version translates the Greek term **paracletos**. The Authorised Version has 'Comforter', the New International Version has 'Counsellor'.

with divine justice on your behalf, pleading your case and securing your acquittal. The Spirit is like a doctor, working inside your sick soul, waking up your conscience to the reality of your sin, revealing Christ and enabling you to accept him as the only Saviour. You could say that Christ is your paraclete in heaven: the Holy Spirit is your paraclete on earth. In all this, the Spirit doesn't act independently of Christ, but on Christ's behalf. It is Christ the king who sends the Holy Spirit to impart to your soul the spiritual blessings secured for you on the cross. So the work of the Son and the Spirit as paracletes is a joint-work.

There is another vital connection between Christ's work and the Spirit's as your two paracletes. As we saw when we looked at prayer and Christ our priest, it's the Holy Spirit who links you into the intercessory ministry the Lord Jesus Christ is carrying out for all his people in heaven. The Spirit takes the desires that are in the heart of Jesus and weaves them into your heart, so that they become your desires too. This living sympathy and harmony of heart between you, praying on earth, and Jesus interceding in heaven, is what gives spiritual effectiveness to your prayers.

There is also a sense in which the Spirit himself intercedes for you. Listen to what Paul says in Romans 8:26, 'Likewise the Spirit helps in our weaknesses. For we do not know what we should pray for as we ought, but the Spirit makes intercession for us with groanings which cannot be uttered.' If the Holy Spirit 'makes intercession for us', does that mean you have two intercessors - Christ in heaven and the Spirit in your heart? Yes: but they are always in perfect agreement with each other. The Holy Spirit pleads within you, not separately from Christ, but by echoing Christ's pleading in heaven. As the Lord Jesus Christ said of the Spirit in another connection, he takes of the things that are Christ's and declares them to Christ's followers (John 16:14). So we could say that the Holy Spirit takes of the heavenly pleading of Christ and declares it within you, by inspiring you to pray with the same holy desires as your heavenly intercessor.

This help of the Holy Spirit in your prayers is essential. If he left you to yourself, you would soon break down under the bruising weight of your burdens. But where you would falter in your human weakness, the Spirit comes; he mingles his divine energies with your own; he lifts you, joins you to Christ, and reproduces in your heart the praying of the heavenly paraclete. Does your spirit feel heavy and sluggish in prayer? Are your burdens too great, so that you stumble about, lost for words? Ask the Holy Spirit to help you.

Come, Holy Spirit, our hearts inspire,
And warm with uncreated fire!

It isn't for nothing that the Bible calls the Holy Spirit 'the Helper'.

The apostle Paul goes on to say in Romans 8:27: 'Now he who searches the hearts knows what the mind of the Spirit is, because he makes intercession for the saints according to he will of God.' There are two important things for you to notice in Paul's teaching here. First, as God searches your praying heart, he recognises in the outpouring of your desires the intercession of his own Holy Spirit. When you are truly praying, your heart is like a spiritual mirror in which God can see himself!

Second, this intercession of the Spirit makes your praying into an open door for God's blessings. This is because the Spirit only asks for things that are 'according to the will of God'. The Holy Spirit is just as much 'God' as the Father and the Son, so he shares all their knowledge; he knows all that lies hidden in the divine purposes. That means he can instil into your heart a desire for the very things God has chosen to give you. In that way, the Holy Spirit, your earthly paraclete, creates a beautiful oneness between God's sovereignty and your prayers. 'The Spirit makes intercession for the saints according to the will of God.' 'This is the confidence we have in him, that if we ask anything according to his will, he hears us' (Romans 8:27, 1 John 5:14).

Points for reflection or discussion

Do you rely on the Holy Spirit to help you to pray? In what ways can you do this?

How can we distinguish between prayers the Holy Spirit inspires, and unspiritual prayers?

Discuss Romans 8:26-7 in the light of what this chapter says about it.

When do you think it would be appropriate to pray **to** the Holy Spirit? Look up the section on the Holy Spirit in one of the older hymn books to see many examples from church history.

13.
What about unanswered prayer?

'You ask and do not receive' (James 4:3).

Over these last few chapters, we're going to look at some of the problems of prayer which we haven't already dealt with. The first one I want us to examine is one of the biggest and most difficult of all: the problem of unanswered prayer.

Unanswered prayer is painful. It can make you doubt whether there's any point in praying at all. You will be especially likely to feel this way if you are going through times of devastating disappointment and sadness. You prayed, expected God to help you, and he failed. So why bother praying any longer?

If that's how you feel, I want to suggest to you that you can probably find an answer to your despairing question in one of three ways.

You may have been praying for the wrong thing.

If you think about it, there are two sorts of things you can pray for. First, you can pray for things which God positively and clearly commands you to pray for in Scripture: for instance, your daily bread and your spiritual growth. As far as these matters are concerned, God's promise applies: 'Ask, and it will be given to you; seek, and you will find; knock, and it will be opened to you' (Matthew 7:7).

It's true that God might sometimes delay his answer even to these petitions. Or he might answer them in such a strange and unexpected way, you hesitate to think that this could actually be God's answer to your prayer. Still, your Christian duty here is simply to believe and pray and wait, until God answers you. He surely will answer, in the time and the way chosen by his own infinite wisdom.

However, there are other cases where you can't be sure what God's will is — where God hasn't revealed in Scripture exactly what he wants you to pray for. In these cases, you have to offer your prayer-requests with total submission to God's sovereignty. If I can put it like this, you must allow your Lord to give or not to give, at his own discretion.

Failure to submit to God's sovereignty in these areas will lead you into all sorts of problems. You may think you know what God ought to do, and how he ought to answer your prayer. You could build up all kinds of arguments in your mind as to why God should do this or that. Perhaps you then come to God in prayer and ask him boldly and confidently to do the thing you are convinced is right. But if God hasn't revealed in his Word that he wants you to pray for that specific thing, your boldness and confidence are merely presumption. You haven't submitted yourself to God's superior wisdom and sovereignty. You've failed to recognise how fallible your own mind is, how easily your prejudices and passions can lead your thinking astray. If God then refuses to grant your prayer, how can you possibly accuse him of letting you down? You may well have been praying for the wrong thing. Absolute submission to God's kingly sovereignty is vital to your prayers, if you are praying about matters where his will isn't certain.

You may have been praying for the right thing, but in a wrong spirit.
The spirit in which you pray is much more important than the things you pray for. In fact, I will go further: the spirit of prayer

is prayer! If you don't pray in a right spirit, you aren't really praying at all; you are just mouthing lot of futile words. You must come to God in a right spirit: a spirit of holy worship, humble dependence and honest confession of sin.

Sadly, Christians don't always approach God to pray in this spirit. We sometimes come thinking only of our own self-centred happiness, not our Lord's glory. We come without any sense of our deep sin or our desperate need of Christ. We come puffed up with arrogance, dictating to the King of the universe, and denying him any right to choose his own time and method of answering us. If that's how we come to God, our hearts are not really praying at all, even though our lips might be asking for the right thing. It is no wonder God doesn't answer us. As far as he is concerned, he is still waiting for us to pray.

You may have misunderstood God's answer to your prayer. This is the commonest mistake we can make. Even though we're praying for the right thing in a right spirit, God doesn't seem to be answering us. We may have misunderstood his answer.

You always need to remember that this life is a kind of spiritual school, in which God is training and preparing you for heaven. The highest possible blessing God can give you here on earth is your sanctification. This is why God sometimes delays to answer your prayers — because he wants to enrich your soul with the inner beauty of patience, humility and hope. Even when he has promised to answer you, he might still make you wait, in order to remind you of your dependence on his sovereign will. When he does finally grant your request, the answer sometimes comes in such a surprising way that you learn deep lessons about your Lord's amazing wisdom and power.

There may be occasions when God refuses to grant your prayers immediately, because an instant 'Yes' would actually not fit in with his good plans. Let me give you an illustration of this from my own experience. I knew a Christian woman who had spent a long time away from home, and was yearning to get back to her family. So she prayed that God would take her safely home and made plans to journey back by ship. But she found that all the places on the ship had already been filled. My homesick friend wept bitter tears when she realised she would have to stay in that far-off place for another two weeks before she could get a ship home. Imagine how she felt when she learned, a few days later, that the ship she'd been planning to take had sunk and everyone on board had drowned. God had really answered my friend's prayer by seeming to deny it; he said 'No' in order to say 'Yes'. To take her safely home, God first had to separate my friend from those whose destiny it was to die on that ship. That was why this Christian woman didn't get an immediate answer to her prayer.

You should also remember that you aren't the only one God takes into account when he answers your prayers. The granting of your request could have quite a complicated relationship with the circumstances of other people. Perhaps things will need to happen in other people's lives, if you are to get a true answer to your request. God may first have to deal with others before he can deal with you.

Sometimes God may perhaps answer your prayers by giving you something better than the thing you prayed for. In this case, the answer comes to you in disguise. You are looking for the blessing in one form, and it arrives in another. You may not even recognise at the time that this is the answer to your prayer. When you do realise it, your heart overflows with gratitude. God's love has done more for you than you asked, giving you a greater and richer blessing than the one you originally desired. 'Now to him who is able to do exceedingly abundantly above all that we ask or think, according to the power that works in us, to him be glory in the church by Christ Jesus throughout all ages, world without end. Amen' (Ephesians 3:20-21).

Points for reflection or discussion

In what sort of ways can we fail to submit to God's superior wisdom and sovereignty, in our prayer as individuals and as a church?

How can we distinguish between boldness and presumption in prayer?

Read the parable of the friend who comes at midnight (Luke 11:5-8). What does it teach about God's delays in answering prayer?

Find examples, in your own life or the lives of others, of a long-delayed answer to prayer which God then granted in a surprising way.

14.

Could all this praying make me into a religious fanatic?

'I am not mad, most noble Festus' (Acts 26:24).

Some Christian are afraid of their religion tipping over into religious fanaticism. That's not surprising when you see the sort of people religious fanatics are; they bring real Christianity into serious disrepute. However, you need not fear that a genuine practice of prayer will turn you into a fanatic. God has placed a number of wise limits around true prayer which stop it from degenerating into a repulsive religious fanaticism.

God's will revealed in Scripture regulates all true prayer. When a religious fanatic prays, he sets aside God's revealed will in the Bible. He claims that he gets special private revelations from God. He then demands that other people must accept these revelations and submit to them; in this way, he sets himself up as a religious authority over others. He won't allow anyone to criticise him or even to investigate his alleged revelations to test their reality.

However, this sort of behaviour contradicts the final and all-sufficient authority of Scripture. Christians are duty-bound to test all doctrines, opinions and experiences by the standard of God's written Word. 'To the law and to the testimony! If they do not speak according to this word, it is because they have no light in them' (Isaiah 8:20). The religious fanatic is putting himself above the Bible when he demands submission to his claims and doesn't like anyone testing them. But the Bible says, 'Test all things' (1 Thessalonians 5:21).

So here is the first barrier that will stop your religion dissolving into the dreams and ravings of the religious fanatic. When you commune with God in prayer, you must submit yourself to the final authority of his written Word. Let the Bible control your thoughts and feelings as you pray.

You must practise self-examination in prayer.

The knowledge of God and the knowledge of yourself are close companions. You can't separate them. The Bible describes God as the one who searches your heart and mind: 'I, the LORD, search the heart, I test the mind, even to give to every man according to his ways, and according to the fruit of his deeds' (Jeremiah 17:10). **You** should be concerned about what's going on in your heart and mind too. With God's help, you ought to practise a careful self-examination.

This is very important in your prayer-life, if you want it to be free from religious fanaticism. The fanatic doesn't really know himself. He has a sinfully deluded idea of who he is and what his motives are. He has convinced himself that he's serving God, whereas in reality he is just serving himself and his own personal glory. His prayers are like those of the Pharisee in Luke 18:9-14; he prays to himself about himself and about how spiritual and close to God he is.

If you want to avoid this cancer of the soul, you need to practise a serious self-examination in your prayers. Before speaking to God, you should sit in judgement on yourself. You should probe into your most secret thoughts and test your heart in the most honest self-inquiry. You will find a lot that distresses you, but this is the only way you can prepare yourself for fruitful fellowship with God. Practise this kind of self-examination, and it will stop your prayers from deteriorating into a self-glorifying religious fanaticism. Instead, you will find yourself becoming a cautious, modest and humble person.

True prayer prevents fanaticism because it recognises Christ's role as Mediator.

When you come before God in genuine worship, you have to lay down your pride and self-importance. You simply aren't good enough to come into God's holy presence by your own excellence. Covered in the filth of your sins, you can only lie in the dust and plead the excellence of another — the Lord Jesus Christ. He, your fair and lovely Mediator, alone makes you and your prayers acceptable to God.

This totally contradicts the spirit of religious fanaticism. The fanatic thinks he is God's favourite, and claims a special position for himself before God. This fills him with a lofty pride, a sense of spiritual superiority. He feels contempt for lesser mortals who don't occupy this exalted position. But true prayer is the opposite of all this. It humbles you deeply with a vast sense of your own unworthiness. It makes you think, not of your own special position, but of your utter dependence on the Lord Jesus Christ's special position. Christ is the one and only Mediator for all unworthy sinners. Praying to the Father through him, you find yourself on the same ground as everyone else. You are no-one special. You are one sinner in a countless company of sinners, all equally relying on the perfection of God's beloved Son. There is no place for a self-exalting religious fanaticism.

From all this, you can see that so far from promoting a spirit of religious fanaticism, real prayer is the best remedy against it.

Points for reflection or discussion

Is it ever right to regard feelings or impressions you receive while praying as special private revelations? How could you test them? Should you demand that others submit to them?

What is the best way of practising self-examination before praying?

In what ways can pride and a sense of spiritual superiority creep into our prayers?

15.
Is prayer consistent with a scientific world-view?

'Whatever the LORD pleases he does, in heaven and in earth, in the seas and in all deep places. He causes the vapours to ascend from the ends of the earth; he makes lightning for the rain; he brings the wind out of his treasuries' (Psalm 135:6-7).

Some people have a problem here which they might express as follows: 'The universe is like a huge, complex machine. Every single event that happens in the universe takes place in accordance with fixed laws built into it by its Creator. Prayer, however, would mean that God is constantly interfering with those laws, making things happen in response to our personal requests. That would upset the whole nature of the universe as a system of scientific law and order.'

People who take this view are throwing up problems, not just for prayer, but for our whole understanding of God. In fact, they are limiting God's sovereign freedom by locking him up as a prisoner of the 'fixed laws' of the universe. They might admit that God created everything in the beginning, but then they shut him out of the daily detailed workings of his world, which (according to them) works by itself, by its own inbuilt laws of cause and effect. The universe is a 'closed system' with which God can't interfere. God becomes a distant spectator, idly watching the machine of the universe going through its clockwork motions.

We must reject this idea of the universe having 'fixed laws' which God can't alter. What we might call the 'laws of nature' are in reality the way that God personally controls his own universe. For example, the law of gravity is simply our way of describing what God normally does when we let go of an object. God wills that the object falls. Or that is what he normally wills. But he is quite free to will otherwise. He is not a slave to the way he normally does things.

So it's wrong to speak of 'fixed laws' of nature, and of God 'interfering' with them. We should see the whole physical universe as a continuous manifestation of God's will and power, as the psalmist did when he wrote the words quoted at the head of this chapter. When we call something a 'law', what we really mean is that that's the way God usually does things. The so-called laws of nature are simply God's customs. If he chooses to act differently — for example, when answering a prayer-request — he isn't breaking any law. He is just varying his routine.

We should also recognise that God can answer our prayers through the way he normally controls the universe. Think about it like this. The world has a spiritual as well as a physical dimension. Humans are the highest beings in this world, and we are spiritual beings; we have souls, and prayer is the soul's highest activity. When God first created the world, he designed it with this great fact in mind. He put the world together in such a way that all its structures and events are secretly organised around its spiritual dimension. In other words, it's part of God's normal control of the world that he governs it in the interests of the human soul and the activity of prayer. That is the most basic 'law' in our world.

It follows that God can answer our prayers through the normal way that the universe operates. We may not understand how, but in a mysterious fashion the physical world and its events have, from the beginning, been tuned into spiritual realities. So God doesn't need to be constantly departing from the way he normally controls the world in order to answer our prayers. His 'normal control' of things has always involved a subordinating of the physical to the spiritual, of matter to soul, of events to prayer.

Points for reflection or discussion

How does a proper understanding of God's sovereignty affect our view of the physical world? Look up some other passages of the Bible that speak about this.

Can we define a miracle as God departing from the way he normally does things? If so, should we expect miracles in response to our prayers? Have you ever experienced a miracle as an answer to prayer?

In view of this close relationship between the physical and the spiritual, how important is what we do with our bodies in prayer?

16.
Should unconverted people pray?

'Let heaven and earth praise him' (Psalm 69:34).

Some Christians may have difficulty here, because they see very clearly that true prayer arises out of a spiritual state of mind. Only the spiritually-minded can pray acceptably to God. So doesn't it follow that an unconverted person, lacking in spiritual-mindedness, will only offend God if he prays? Wouldn't it be better for him not to pray until he is converted?

It sounds plausible, but there is a problem. This argument really means that the lack of a true spiritual **desire** to pray frees us from the **obligation** to pray. Our very sinfulness becomes our reason for not doing what we ought to do. No-one can accept such a wicked idea.

If you go back to the opening chapters and look at the aspects of prayer we outlined there, it should be obvious that it is everyone's duty to pray. Shouldn't everyone adore and praise God? Shouldn't all human beings express their dependence on their Creator through petition and thanksgiving? Shouldn't all sinners confess their sins and pray for forgiveness and liberation? Shouldn't we all love one another and express that love by interceding for one another? An unconverted person can't claim that he is free from the obligation to do these things. He can't say, 'I'm unconverted, so it isn't my duty to adore or praise God, depend on God, or confess my sins.' But if it is the unconverted person's duty to do these things, it is his duty to pray, because all these things are aspects of prayer.

What about the argument that an unconverted person's prayers are unacceptable to God because he prays out of an unspiritual mind? That goes back to what I said before: it really means that his sinfulness frees him from his duty. 'My lack of spiritual-mindedness excuses me from my obligation to worship God, depend on God, and confess my sins.' No, it doesn't! If you think about it for a moment, you will see how utterly false this idea is.

Suppose someone had just got married and then said to his wife, 'Woman, I'm under no obligation to love you or care for you, because I am by nature a selfish man who has no regard for the rights of others. My selfish nature frees me from my duty to love you.' No woman would think that a very good excuse for wife-beating. It's the same in our relationship with God. Prayer is of the essence of that relationship. To refuse to pray on the grounds of our personal ungodliness is to insult God twice over. We are sinfully unwilling to pray, and we make our sinful unwillingness into our excuse for not praying. It's a wicked excuse!

If we could excuse ourselves from praying because we lack the desire, then we would be free from the claims of all goodness for the same reason. We could say, 'I have no real desire to be fair-minded, truthful, compassionate or self-controlled. Therefore I am under no obligation to practise these virtues.' What is this but making sin into its own excuse? It would leave us free to practise every kind of evil without any blame attaching to us, and without any duty to reform ourselves or repent. The whole idea is devilish. It contradicts the clearest testimony of our consciences. No matter how sinful we are, we **know** that we ought to obey God. No amount of depravity can ever cancel that absolute obligation.

So if you are not yet a Christian, even while you remain unconverted, it is still your duty to pray: to adore, praise, petition and thank your Creator, to confess your sins and ask his forgiveness, and to intercede for others. It is true that your unconverted heart cannot do these things in a spiritual way that pleases God. But not to do them at all is even worse. Best of all is for you to confess to God the sinfulness of having an unconverted heart, and to pray for your own conversion through the saving power of the Lord Jesus Christ and the Holy Spirit. Then your prayers will become acceptable to God; you will have a renewed mind, you will have a true desire to pray, and the perfect righteousness of Jesus Christ, God's beloved Son, your great high priest, will cover and hide all your remaining sinfulness.

Points for reflection or discussion

In what ways should we encourage unbelievers to see their duty to worship God and depend on him? What if they don't even believe in God?

Even as Christians we can sometimes lack the desire to pray. How would this chapter's advice apply to us then?

We don't often hear preachers today exhorting unbelievers to pray for their own conversion. Yet this was common once. Why has it gone out of fashion today?

Part two

Profiting from Prayer

An abridged rewrite of
'The return of prayers'
by Thomas Goodwin (1600-1680)

Prepared by David Harman

Dedicated, in gratitude to God, to the memory of
Miss Stephanie Wright
(former Librarian of the Evangelical Library)
who first proposed an abridgement of
The Return of Prayers
and began the work until her sudden death in a
tragic road accident in 1990.

Contents

Chapter   **Page**

Introduction

Thomas Goodwin (1600-1680), a Congregationalist, was one of Oliver Cromwell's top advisers and served under that general's appointment as president of Magdalen College, Oxford. Early in his career Goodwin was recognized as 'a Puritan divine of very superior powers, whose writings cast much light on the Scriptures'. In *The Return of Prayers* Goodwin is at his best, expounding with clarity and insight the words of Psalm 85:8: 'I will listen to what God the LORD will say; he promises peace to his people, his saints — but let them not return to folly'.

Goodwin wrote this book to help Christians become more convinced of the value of prayer and to persevere in it. Some Christians give up praying because they feel that God is not answering their prayers. Others are perplexed by God's answering them in a different way from what they expect. Some believers do not take the trouble to observe God's answers and thereby lose comfort and blessing. This book will be a help to all such.

Goodwin's original work is in three sections:
1. Listening to what God has to say.
2. God speaking peace.
3. The folly of relapsing.

This abridged work is concerned with the first section only. It follows Goodwin's original chapter divisions. Scripture quotations are taken from the New International Version of the Bible.

Psalm 85 prophesies the return of the Jews from Babylonian captivity. It is also a prayer that God's people might once again enjoy their former blessings. The psalmist urges the Lord to be gracious to his Church, recalling to mind former deliverances. Then, having finished his prayer, he awaits an answer from heaven. 'I will listen to what God will say', he says.

D. G. H.

1.
God's people are to take careful note of the answers to their prayers.

Firstly, when we have prayed to God we can be sure that he will answer us. 'My God will hear me', says the prophet Micah (Micah 7:7). 'I will look to see what he will say to me', says Habakkuk (Hab. 2:1). Why should we do this? Because we shall despise God's gracious provision for us if we think that prayer will not be any use in bringing about the purpose for which God has ordained it. Every faithful prayer is ordained by God to be a means of obtaining what we desire and pray for. 'This is the assurance we have in approaching God: that if we ask anything according to his will, he hears us' (1 John 5:14). It is true that God hears an enemy, but this is not the kind of meaning we are talking about. God hears his people's prayers with *favour*. God's ears are said to be *open* to their prayers, and so John follows his statement by saying in the next verse, 'And if we know he hears us — whatever we ask — we know that we have what we asked of him' (1 John 5:15). Our prayers are granted as soon as we have prayed, even though the process of fulfilling our requests has not yet begun. As soon as a godly man prays, the prayer instantaneously arrives in heaven and the petition is immediately granted. As soon as Daniel prayed, an answer was given, although the angel that brought that message did not arrive until some time later (Daniel 9:20-23). No prayer is ever useless. Where God has given a heart to speak, he has an ear to hear. To think otherwise is to despise God's gracious provision for us.

Secondly, if we are not confident that our prayer is going to be heard, not only is God's provision for us misused, but his name is misused also. You evidently think God's arm is too short to save or his ear too dull to hear. You thus rob God of one of his most royal titles, for he describes himself as 'a God that hears prayer'. You should remember that the petitions of God's people do not pass out of his sight until he sends an answer. After David had prayed he said that he waited for an answer more than watchmen wait for the morning (Psalm 130:6). Elsewhere, David says, 'Morning by morning, O LORD, you hear my voice; morning by morning I lay my requests before you and wait in expectation' (Psalm 5:3). He expected an answer.

Thirdly, if God gives you an answer and you take no notice of it, you let God speak to you in vain. That is a great insult to God. Our speaking to God in prayer and his answering us form a great part of our experience of walking with God. We should study his dealings with us and compare our prayers with his answers. In 1 Kings 8:56 Solomon stated that not one word had failed of all God's good promises. We should regard our prayers as a way of putting God's promises into action.

Again, if you do not wait for the Lord to speak you will provoke him not to answer you at all. God will see that it will be quite useless for him to answer. It is not enough just to pray. After you have prayed you need to listen for an answer, so that you may receive what you have prayed for. Otherwise, you will not observe God fulfilling your prayers. How then will you bless God and give him thanks for hearing you?

Watchfulness and thankfulness are required in prayer (Colossians 4:2). Perhaps the reason you pray so much and give thanks so little is because you take such little notice of God's answers. When we have offered a faithful prayer, God is made our debtor because of his promises. We are to take note of his payment and give him a receipt. Otherwise, God loses some of the praise due to him.

As God will then be the loser thereby, so will you be a loser. You will lose the experience you might have had through it — an experience of God and his faithfulness. If you have proved God again and again in answering your prayers such experiences will give you hope and confidence in God at other times. David says, 'Because he turned his ear to me, I will call upon him as long as I live' (Psalm 116:2). It is as if he had said, 'Now that God has heard me, I know where to go. This experience, even if I had no more, is enough to encourage me to go on praying to God'.

Furthermore, by observing God's answers to your prayers, you will gain an insight into your own heart, ways and prayers, and learn how to judge them. David's assurance that he did not have sinful desires in his heart was strengthened by God's having heard his prayers. He reasons thus, 'If I had cherished sin in my heart, the Lord would not have listened, but God has surely listened and heard my voice in prayer' (Psalm 66:18-19). If God does not answer your petitions it will make you enquire as to the reason for it. You will then examine your prayers and the state of your heart to see whether, in fact, you had prayed with wrong motives (see James 4:3). If you have a friend who is usually punctual in answering your letters but who then fails to answer you in a particular matter, you begin to think that something must be wrong. You then take steps to find out what has caused the delay. Perhaps you have offended your friend in some way. It is like this with your prayers. If you do not take careful note of answers to prayer you will lose much comfort. There is no greater joy than seeing prayers answered. 'Ask and you will receive, and your joy will be complete', says Jesus (John 16:24). As it is a great joy to see anyone converted, it is an even greater joy to the one who has been the means of it. To see God do much good to his Church, and hear others' prayers for it, is a comfort. How much more is it a joy to see

God do it as a result of one's own prayers! That God and we should be of one mind and desire the same things is a cause for great joy. It is wonderful when we see that we ourselves have been answered. You lose much comfort and blessing when you do not take note of the answers to your prayers.

2.

How to find out God's intentions towards you when you pray.

How do you recognize answers to your prayers and how do you know when God is taking action in response to them?

Firstly, you must be content to see some prayers never answered in your own lifetime. For example, the fulfilment of your prayers for the utter downfall of God's enemies and the flourishing of the Gospel must wait for the Church to reap in years to come. Such prayers will not be lost. If they are offered up by the eternal Spirit they have eternal significance. For instance, the prayer that Stephen made for his persecutors, Acts 7:60, was fulfilled after his death in the conversion of Saul of Tarsus. David's prayer against his enemy in Psalm 109:8-9 had its final fulfilment about a thousand years later in the downfall of Judas (Acts 1:20). When the prophets predicted the sufferings of Christ and the glories that would follow, it was revealed to them that they were not serving themselves, but us (1 Peter 1:10-12). So in prayer, if we pray with the guidance of the Holy Spirit, we may ask for many things that will come to pass much later. Perhaps God will reveal to you by a secret impression on your spirit that he will use your prayers, among others, for the accomplishment of his purposes in days to come. In this way God gives you an assurance that he has accepted you as belonging to him.

God never revealed his love more to Moses than when he prayed for God's people. One of the best evidences of the uprightness of your heart is that you can pray for the good of the Church for a long time to come, even though you may never see it with your own eyes. When you reach heaven your joy will be full when you see that your prayers have resulted in the conversion of those for whom you prayed, and the ruin of the Church's enemies. There is joy in heaven over one sinner who repents. Similarly, those whose prayers are used by God in any matter will have great reason to rejoice in heaven!

3.
How God answers prayer for our relatives, friends and temporal blessings.

We are commanded to pray for others. See, for example, James 5:16 and 1 John 5:16. How are such prayers answered? We know that such prayers are often granted. Why else would God make promises concerning them? God gives us promises to encourage us to pray and to witness his abundant love for us. It is a sign that we are in extraordinary favour with God when he hears us, and an evidence of our priesthood. We have this favour through the fellowship we have with Christ as our High Priest. God has made us kings and priests to prevail and intercede for others. If God hears prayers for others, how much more will he hear us for our own needs? When Christ healed the paralytic in Matthew 9:2 it is recorded that he took note of the faith of those who brought the man to him. This scripture is intended to encourage us to bring others to the Lord in prayer.

Our prayers for others, however, may often not be answered in the way we hoped. Samuel's prayer for Saul was not granted (Compare 1 Samuel 15:11 with verse 35). Prayer is like other means that God has instituted for the good of others. We may preach to many and yet few may believe. Similarly, we may pray for many, not knowing who are appointed to receive eternal life. However, although we do not know what will happen, we are still to pray for them (1 Timothy 2:1-4). Where God gives opportunity for preaching it is more than likely that he has some people to convert. Usually the Word of God takes root among some, though often in but a few.

In the same way, when God has stirred up our hearts to pray for others it is a sign that he will hear us for at least some of them. God may, in his wisdom, deny our requests for some. God requires us to pray out of duty, because prayer is a means ordained by him through which he often brings things to pass. However, God has not bound himself to answer every prayer in exactly the same way as we have asked. Although God's promise to hear and accept prayer is general and universal, yet his promise to hear it by granting the very thing itself prayed for is only indefinite. God makes similar promises concerning other means of doing men good, such as our reproofs or our preaching. For example, the promise of healing in James 5:15 cannot be universal. If the promise were universal we might conclude that sick men for whom prayer had been made would never die. But we know it is appointed for all men to die. This Scripture in James is a provision to which God has attached a gracious promise, because he often does restore the sick through prayer, although not in every case. On any particular occasion we must rely upon God to fulfil his promises, quietly resting upon his Word. We cannot, however, have a full assurance that we shall obtain everything we ask for, because the promise is not universal, but indefinite.

This can be illustrated by reference to other promises of a temporal or outward nature. There is a promise of long life to those who honour their parents, yet we know from experience and from the Scripture that it does not always turn out that way. This particular promise, therefore, cannot be absolute, infallible or universal, but only indefinite.

While we must approach such promises in faith, we must do so quietly resting in God and in submission to his will. We must submit to God's good pleasure as to the way he disposes of the matter. Faith must embrace the promises in general in full belief that God means what he has said, and that he certainly will fulfil his promises according to his purpose. However, we must not assume that in any particular instance God's promises will be fulfilled to us in exactly the same way as we have asked. The truth, purpose and intent of the promise is not universal, but indefinite. What God requires of us is not an absolutely full persuasion that he will perform a promise to us in any particular manner. God requires only an act of dependence, quietly resting in his will. Nevertheless, if God should at any time give us a special faith concerning any particular temporal blessing for ourselves or others, we may be certain that we shall receive it.

When God gave the apostles power to work miracles, they were bound to believe that the miracles would without fail be performed by them, as in the case of casting out demons. Thus Jesus on one occasion rebukes them for lack of faith in this respect (Matthew 17:19-20). It is in this way that Jesus' words in Matthew 21:21-22 are to be understood: 'If you have faith and do not doubt ... you can say to this mountain, "Go, throw yourself into the sea", and it will be done. If you believe, you will receive whatever you ask for in prayer'. When God works in us such a faith we must believe with absolute certainty that the thing will be done, and it shall be done. But God does not always call us to such a kind of special faith. If God did stir up such a faith, he would accomplish the thing asked for but, in general, promises made about outward things are not universal, but indefinite. We cannot, therefore, believe with absolute certainty that God is under obligation to bestow any temporal blessing on ourselves or others in response to our prayers.

When we pray for others and yet God does not see fit to grant that particular blessing, then although our prayers seem to be returned to us unanswered, they will return for our good. In Psalm 35:12-13, David said that he prayed for his enemies when they were sick but that his prayers were returned to him unanswered. In his prayers, David showed the sincerity of his heart towards God and his true forgiveness of his enemies. Although his prayer did not profit his enemies, it turned to David's own good. It came back with blessings for himself. God stirs up in his children this willingness to pray for their enemies, but he does not always mean to answer those prayers in the way that has been asked. He means to draw forth and reward those holy attitudes of heart which are the noblest part of God's image in his children and with which he is so much delighted.

If we have prayed for long for those whom God does not intend to bless, he will in the end remove our desire to pray for them. What God did by a revelation from heaven to Samuel (1 Samuel 16:1) and to Jeremiah (Jeremiah 7:16), he does now by a less obvious method. He will withdraw the Holy Spirit's assistance in prayer. God does this because he is loath not to hear his people when they pray. When God does not mean to hear, he lays the key of prayer out of the way, so desirous is he to give answers to every prayer.

Sometimes God will let us pray for the conversion or good of someone he does not intend to bless. He does this to show that his thoughts are not the same as ours, for he may then answer those prayers in the life of some other person. This will give us as much joy as if he had answered us according to our original intent. Abraham prayed for Ishmael, but God gave him Isaac instead (Genesis 17:18-19). You may perhaps pray for one person more than another out of natural affection. God, however, may answer you by blessing another for whom, perhaps, your heart was not so much stirred. When the latter is converted, it proves to be as great a comfort as if the former for whom you had prayed had been blessed.

4.

How we may know what influence our own prayers have had in bringing events to pass.

How may we know what effect our own contribution has made when we have joined with others in prayer? Satan is apt to object that, although the prayer was answered, it was not due to any contribution from ourselves. The answers are:

1. If you wholeheartedly joined with others in praying, then it is certain that your voice helped to make it effectual. Jesus said, 'If two of you on earth agree about anything you ask for, it will be done for you by my Father in heaven' (Matthew 18:19). The word 'agree' here has the meaning of harmoniously playing the same tune. Prayers are music in God's ears. The meaning is that it is not simply being of the same mind about the thing that is prayed for that is important; the emotions are also involved. It is the emotions that make the ensemble and the melody. Now if the same holy emotions are aroused by God's Spirit in your heart as in others, then you help to make up the ensemble. Indeed, without your voice, the melody would be incomplete. Especially is this so when, without your knowing, others were praying for the same thing. Then surely your prayers have had an effect as well as those of others.

2. God often provides evidence in several ways that a person's prayers have contributed to the fulfilment of something.

(a) God may so order it that a person who has prayed most for a matter has the first news of its fulfilment. Simeon had surely been most earnest in asking the Lord to send the Messiah into the world and to restore his people Israel. God had revealed to him that he should not die until he had seen the Christ for himself. So, to give Simeon evidence of God's regard for his prayers, God brought the old man into the temple at exactly the same time as the child was brought to be presented to the Lord (Luke 2:27-28). Anna, who had served God with fastings and prayers night and day, also came into the temple at exactly the same time (Luke 2:36-38). By some such circumstances or other God often witnesses to our hearts that he has heard our prayers along with those of other people.

(b) God may fill the heart with much joy in the fulfilment of what has been prayed for. This is a powerful evidence that our prayers, as well as those of others, moved the Lord to bring the matter to pass. Simeon was so overjoyed that he was even willing to die when he saw the answer to his prayers. If you have a thankful heart for a blessing received by someone for whom you joined with others in prayer, it is a sign that your prayers contributed to the result.

(c) God may stir you up to pray for yourself and incline others to do the same for you. If these prayers are heard then God most certainly had regard to your *own* prayers, even more than to the prayers of others who prayed for you.

5.
How God helps us in our praying.

When God wants us to pray he creates a praying frame of mind. He creates motives, and suggests arguments and pleas to bring before God. Along with this we find a warming of our hearts, a lingering, a longing, and a restlessness of spirit to be alone and to pour out the soul before God. We must take careful note of such times and not neglect them, for it is certain that we then have God's ear. It is a special opportunity for prayer, such as we may never have again. The psalmist says, 'You hear, O LORD, the desire of the afflicted; you encourage them, and you listen to their cry' (Psalm 10:17). It is a great sign that God means to hear you when he stirs up your petitions in this way.

We should, however, note the difference between God's work and Satan's in this respect. Satan will often make unreasonable suggestions and urgings to pray, such as when we are working, or need to eat or sleep. He especially uses this device to tire out new converts. The difference is that the devil comes in a violent and imperious manner upon the conscience, but does not in the slightest way prepare the heart to pray. On the other hand, if God calls us to prayer at such extraordinary times, he fits and prepares the heart for it. He fills the soul with holy desires and gives the ability to do the thing he calls for. When God will have any great matters done, he sets his people's hearts to work at prayer by a kind of gracious instinct.

He stirs them up and moves their hearts by the influence of his Holy Spirit. When Daniel knew from the Scriptures that the time of Judah's captivity was drawing to an end, he was stirred up to seek God for it (Daniel 9:2). This was just what God had said would happen. Through Jeremiah, God said that he would bring about the return of his people to their own land. 'When seventy years are completed for Babylon, I will come to you and fulfil my gracious promise to bring you back to this place ... then you will call upon me and pray to me, and I will listen to you. You will seek me and find me when you seek me with all your heart. I will be found by you, declares the LORD' (Jeremiah 29:10-14). We ought therefore to take careful note of the times when God especially moves our hearts to pray.

Sometimes, we may have no thoughts of praying for any particular thing, but God stirs us up to pray, drawing us into his presence and moving us to call upon him. When God thus calls us to prayer it is a sure sign that he intends to hear us.

There are also other ways in which we may be sure God will hear us.

1. When God quiets, calms and contents the heart in prayer, this is a good sign. Paul prayed earnestly for God to take away the thorn in his flesh. He said he pleaded with the Lord three times for it. God, however, assured Paul that his grace was sufficient for him and that his power was made perfect in weakness. This calmed the mind of the apostle (2 Corinthians 12: 7-9). You may have been praying for a long time for God to relieve some distress, and God comforts you with a promise like this, 'I will never leave you nor forsake you'. This quiets and contents the mind. This is God's answer, and you must take note of such answers, for they are precious.

2. When God draws near and reveals his love to you in prayer it is a token that he hears you regarding that particular request. You must take special note of this, for God, in smiling upon you and welcoming you, indicates not only that he hears your prayer, but that he accepts your person. Isaiah says, 'You will call and the LORD will answer: you will cry for help, and he will say, "Here I am"' (Isaiah 58:9). There may be times when you will no sooner come into God's presence to enquire of him, but he says, 'Here I am'. When God draws near in this way it is a sure sign that he hears you.

Daniel had fasted and prayed for three weeks, when a heavenly messenger came and told him he was highly esteemed and that his words were heard from the very first day (Daniel 10:11-12). Similarly, when God by his Spirit comes down, meets you and tells you secretly that you are his beloved and he is yours, then your prayers are certainly heard. If he accepts you as a person, how much more does he accept your prayers.

A word of caution is needed, however. This is not always an infallible sign that a particular request will be granted, although the prayer is accepted. It is certainly an evidence that your prayer is heard. Even what you ask is agreeable to God's will and he greatly approves of you and of your request. If God then so draws near, why does he not mean to grant the request? The answer is that God *approves* of many things that he does not *decree*. God has an approving will and a decretive will. God may show his approving will of the thing you ask by drawing near in the way described. Let us suppose that you have been asking for something which is of great importance to the Church. God shows his approval for your encouragement, yet it does not necessarily follow that he has decreed to do that particular thing. His revealing of himself is often the only answer he intended to such a prayer. It is answer enough to enjoy the assurance of God's love.

You may have prayed against some evil which you see coming upon the Church. God may still intend to bring that evil, but because he set your heart to pray against it, thereby demonstrating your own sincerity, he draws near. He tells you that it shall go well with you and that you are greatly beloved by him. Sometimes this is the only answer God intends to give. Sometimes he does this to content the heart and prepare it for a denial. Otherwise, the denial of what you had been earnest about might cause you to question or doubt God's love.

3. It is a good sign when God stirs up a particular confidence about something, upholding us to wait for it in spite of all discouragements. This he did for David in Psalm 27. David was then in great danger from Saul or Absalom, and so frequently that to all outward probability he was never likely to live quietly in Jerusalem again. David, however, prayed about this and made it the grand request of his whole life. He said. 'One thing I ask of the LORD, this is what I seek: that I may dwell in the house of the LORD all the days of my life' (Psalm 27:4). God granted him a special faith that it would be so, for he had said previously, in verse 3. 'Though an army besiege me, my heart will not fear; though war break out against me, even then I will be confident'. David's faith was vindicated. By means of prayer our hearts may be particularly strengthened and assured that God will certainly act. This is rare and extraordinary, but by no means unknown.

A caution is also required here. The thing prayed for does not always come to pass. Those persuasions stirred up by God may be, and often are, conditional upon obedience. In the case of Eli's family, God said, 'I promised that your house and your father's house would minister before me for ever'. But God went on to say, 'Far be it from me! Those who honour me I will honour, but those who despise me will be disdained' (1 Samuel 2:30). Eli's sons had broken the condition which was implied in the promise and so they forfeited the blessings.

4. It is also a good sign when God creates a restless persistence in spite of all discouragements. As above, when David said, 'One thing I ask, this is what I will seek', he did not stop seeking God for it. Jesus taught the same truth in the parable of the persistent widow (Luke 18:1-8). Note, however, that it is possible to be persistent out of an unseemly desire. It is possible to ask with wrong motives, and then we shall not get what we ask (James 4:3). However, if our persistence is joined to a subjection to God's will, then it is God who has stirred it up and we may confidently expect an answer.

6.

The importance of the state of our hearts after prayer.

You must make sure that you have an obedient and dependant heart. If God keeps you in a more obedient frame of spirit after praying it is a sign that he intends to answer you. By contrast, David said, 'If I had cherished sin in my heart, the Lord would not have listened; but God has surely listened and heard my voice in prayer' (Psalm 66:18-19). That consideration acted as a curb upon David so that he was careful not to sin. If we are careless about the way we view sin, this provokes God and we shall lose whatever we might otherwise have gained by praying.

On another occasion, in Psalm 143, when David was in danger of losing his life, he especially prayed that God would direct him and keep him. David knew that, if he sinned, all his prayers would be spoilt. So, after praying that God would rescue him from his enemies, he prayed, 'Teach me to do you will, for you are my God; may your good Spirit lead me on level ground' (Psalm 143:10). This was more important to him than his deliverance. When God meant to give David the kingdom God kept him innocent and his heart tender. (See 1 Samuel 24:1-7).

You must continue to hope in God and for the fulfilment of your requests, telling the Lord that you are waiting for and expecting an answer. This is a sign that the answer is on the way. David said, 'I am still confident of this: I will see the goodness of the LORD in the hand of the living. Wait for the LORD; be strong and take heart and wait for the LORD (Psalm 27:13-14). The hope and expectation of a godly man would make him ashamed if they were not fulfilled. Answers are therefore sure to come, and are implied by these words, 'Wait on the LORD and keep his way. He will exalt you ...' (Psalm 37:34).

7.

How we may know whether the fulfilment of a matter was due to prayer or to common Providence?

We are prone to look upon what are truly answers to prayer as the mere outworkings of common providence. How can we discern true answers to prayer?

1. When God does something in answer to prayer he often does it in such a manner that it is unmistakable. When God hears prayers that have been a long while in the making, he usually shows half a miracle one way or the other. God shows his hand in answers to prayer in many ways:

(a) Many obstacles and difficulties may lie in the way of an answer. If they are removed, God making a key on purpose (as it were) to unlock the door, it is a sign that this is the result of prayer. There are many examples of this in the Bible: David's coming to the kingdom; Joseph's being brought out of prison; Mordecai's being exalted to honour; Peter's being released from prison. The last is a most remarkable case. Peter was sleeping between two soldiers. If they had awaked, he would have been discovered. He was in chains, but they fell off. There were guards at the door, but they took no notice. An iron gate flew open of its own accord.

2. When God uses a combination of factors like these to bring an event to pass, the lack of any one of which would have made

it impossible, then it is prayer that has done it. When God delivered the people of Israel from Egypt, their captors came themselves at midnight and begged them to go, even encouraging them with gifts of jewellery. Pharaoh himself dismissed them courteously and fairly, desiring their prayers that God would bless him also. Not a dog moved its tongue, so that not even those brute creatures disturbed Israel, during the night, when they would usually have been most troublesome.

3. When God brings about a sudden and unexpected accomplishment of something that has been long prayed for, perhaps even before we are aware of it, it is obviously an answer to prayer. In the previous examples, Peter was asleep and was not even dreaming of a deliverance. In Joseph's release from prison and his advancement to be the greatest in the kingdom, the suddenness of it all showed that God had remembered him and had answered his prayers.

4. When God grants more than we asked for, this is also a sign that he has heard our prayers. Paul said that God 'is able to do immeasurably more than all we ask or imagine' (Ephesians 3:20). Solomon asked for wisdom, but God gave him more than he asked for: peace, riches, and honour, as well as wisdom (1 Kings 3:12-13). Hannah asked for one son only, but God gave her three sons and two daughters (1 Samuel 1:10 and 2:21). When prayers are answered, blessings usually come densely packed; they come tumbling in. The thing prayed for does not come alone.

5. When something is granted by prayer, there is often some particular circumstance or providence along with it which is a token for good, and is a seal that it is from God. When prayer had been made for a wife for Isaac, God gave a remarkable sign that the prayers had been heard. Abraham's servant had prayed in particular that the young woman who arrived to draw water,

and who, in response to his request offered drink not only to him but to his camels also, would be the one God had appointed for Isaac. And Rebekah, being the first to arrive, spoke those selfsame words (Gen. 24:12-19). This was a clear indication of God's hand in the matter and so the servant bowed down and worshipped the Lord (verse 26).

Again, a consideration of the timing of the granting of our requests may help much to discern whether they are answers to prayer. God shows his wisdom and love as much in the timing as in the giving of the thing itself. God said through Isaiah, 'In the time of my favour I will answer you' (Isaiah 49:8). David said that he prayed to the LORD in the time of God's favour (Psalm 69:13). God answers in the best and most acceptable time for us. He longs to be gracious, for he is a God of justice (Isaiah 30:18). He is a wise God and knows the fittest times and seasons in which to show kindness and dispense his favours. Sometimes the matter is accomplished at about the same time in which we are most urgent in prayer. God said through Isaiah, 'Before they call I will answer; and while they are still speaking I will hear' (Isaiah 65:24). When Peter was in prison, he came and knocked at the door at the precise moment when the Church was gathered together to pray for him (Acts 12: 5-16). When Jesus healed the royal official's son, the man found that it was precisely when Jesus said to him, 'Your son lives', that he got better (John 4:46-54).

In answering prayer, God aims especially at two things, Firstly, God wishes to show his mercy so that we might be humbly grateful for his undeserved kindness to us. Secondly, God wishes to have our hearts satisfied and full of joy and contentment with the answer, so that we may delight in God's goodness. For these two purposes he brings together the times when we have most need with those when we are most receptive to him and our sinful desires are subdued. We are then most fit to relish God's goodness alone and not liable to be drawn away with the sensual appeal of the thing prayed for.

116

Suppose you have prayed for a long time for assurance of salvation and joy in the Holy Spirit. When you have most need of it, (perhaps when you have seen great trouble approaching), then God has answered. This was the fittest time for God to have heard your prayer.

In the previous example of Peter, it is clear that he had been in prison for some time. God could have delivered him at any time in answer to the prayers of the Church. But God kept Peter in prison until that very night before the morning when Herod meant to bring Peter out for execution. That was the fittest time for God to answer. If what you have prayed for comes to pass when you have abandoned all other considerations and have cast yourself upon God alone, then that was the fittest time for God to act.

There is another way you may know whether a matter is granted in answer to prayer. God may deal with you in proportion to your dependence upon him and according to the closeness of your walk with him. David said, 'To the faithful you show yourself faithful, to the blameless you show yourself blameless, to the pure you show yourself pure, but to the crooked you show yourself shrewd' (Psalm 18:25-26). When Moses' hands were down, the Amalekites were winning; but when his hands were lifted up, the Israelites were winning (Exodus 17:11). It is possible to start praying earnestly for something only to dash all prospects of an answer by falling into some sin. God would have us observe that there is a connection between our attitude towards him and answers to prayer.

8.
Observations on the effect that answers to prayers have on our hearts.

If the thing granted draws your heart nearer to God then it is certain that it was granted in answer to prayer. Things obtained by prayer are made holy to us and in that way they will not ensnare or entangle our hearts. Anything obtained by prayer we should return to God and use it for God's glory. Having obtained Samuel by prayer, Hannah dedicated him to God (1 Samuel 1:27-28). Prayers answered will produce thankfulness. If the Holy Spirit stirs you up to thankfulness it is a sure sign that he was the author of your prayer. Prayer and thanks are like the double movement of the lungs; the air that is sucked in by prayer is breathed out by thanks.

Again, if the blessings obtained encourage you to go to God another time and to pray more confidently and fervently, it is a sign that you received the former by prayer. The Psalmist said, 'I love the LORD, for he heard my voice; he heard my cry for mercy. Because he turned his ear to me, I will call on him as long as I live' (Psalm 116:1-2).

Again, if you are stirred up to pay vows that were made as you were asking God for a particular blessing, you preserve the memory of the receipt of that blessing. It is an evidence that the blessing was obtained by prayer if God stirs you up to perform those vows.

If you can see by faith that God's hand was in the accomplishment of the matter rather than second causes, and can acknowledge that to his glory, this is because he has heard your prayers. God's intention in hearing prayer is that we might glorify him.

Then again, if with the blessing there comes an assurance of God's love and an evidence of his favour, you will then know well enough that it was the result of prayer.

Lastly, the proof will be in the event itself. Things obtained by prayer have few thorns in them; the curse is taken out. On the other hand, what comes by ordinary providences may come with many troubles. The reason is that what comes by prayer comes as a blessing, and so no trouble is added to it (Proverbs 10:22). Prayer also kills those excessive desires which cause so much vanity and vexation in our enjoyments. Things deferred but at last obtained by prayer prove most enjoyable and comforting.

9.
How to remain quiet and discern an answer to prayer when what has been prayed for is not granted.

This is a difficult matter. How shall we know that God has heard prayer if the thing itself is not granted? This is often the case. Christ prayed that, if it were possible, the cup might pass from him, yet we know that it was not the Father's will that it should (Matthew 26:39, 42). How do we reconcile this with the teaching in Romans 8:26 that the Holy Spirit intercedes for us when we do not know what we ought to pray? If the Holy Spirit knows that God will not grant our request, why would he stir us up to pray? You would think that the Spirit, who knows the mind of God, would always guide our hearts aright and not let us err or miss in the things we pray for. The answer is, firstly, that the Holy Spirit does not produce prayers in us according to what God's *secret* will and foreknowledge is, but according to what God's *revealed* will is. God's revealed will is presented to us both in his Word and in his providence. God leads us to pray, not always according to his secret will, but according to what is our duty to pray for most. This is similar to God's method in using preaching. God knows whom he means to convert, yet he often assists preachers to preach as much to those he does not intend to convert as to those he does mean to convert. God deals with us in these things according to what our duty is and not according to what is his decree.

Secondly, in Romans 8:26 it is said that the Spirit helps us in our *weakness*. He does not help us according to his vast knowledge, but helps our infirm, weak and narrow understanding. In this way he stirs up in us such things as, *according to our knowledge*, we have a duty to seek from God. These will be things that we consider to be most for our good and for God's glory. God accepts such desires yet does for us according to the largeness of his own love. How, then, do we deal with the problem of seemingly unanswered prayer?

The first thing is our attitude in prayer. Did we pray for something absolutely and assertively simply because we regarded it as best for ourselves? If so, we must not be surprised if the prayer is denied. We abused our privilege. But if we prayed conditionally, and with an 'if', as Christ did, and with a 'not my will, but yours be done', we are to rest in God's judgement as to what is best for us. We can then interpret the prayer as answered in spite of the denial.

We should also understand that sometimes the denial of a godly person's prayer is for his greater good and is laid as a foundation for a greater blessing. Sometimes the very denial may break your heart and bring you nearer to God. You will then begin to search your ways to see if there is something wrong with your prayers or with your general attitude. This in itself can be a great blessing. If by the loss of one thing we learn how to pray better we may be able to obtain a hundred better things afterwards. Christ prayed that the cup might pass (Matthew 26:39,42). It did not pass, but that denial was the foundation of our salvation and the way to Christ's glory.

We should also be aware of the possibility that there may be a turning of the thing desired into some other greater blessing of the same kind. All God's ways are mercy and truth to his people and God improves, collects and lays out the precious stocks of their prayers to the best advantage. God has an eye to where the greatest returns and gains may accrue. Jacob did not lay his hands of blessing as Joseph intended but crossed his hands and so blessed the younger son rather than the elder (Gen. 48:17-19). Similarly, the blessing that Isaac intended for Esau was transferred to Jacob. It was not lost (Genesis 27). There can be transfers of this sort which are not to be seen as denials but as true answers to prayer.

Again, our prayers may be answered according to their main thrust even though the actual things asked for are not received. God answers according to the hinge upon which prayer turns. We may perceive something which we feel would be much for God's glory, the good of the Church and our own comfort and happiness. God may not grant that request specifically, but because his glory was uppermost in our desires, that prayer will most certainly be answered, although in some other way. David had a great desire to build a house for the LORD, and the LORD commended him because it was in his heart to do such a thing. Nevertheless God did not permit David himself to build the temple; that honour was given to David's son, Solomon (1 Kings 8:17-18). Sometimes, although God denies a request, he may lean a considerable way towards it in order to give satisfaction to his child. Abraham prayed earnestly for Ishmael and God went as far in granting his request as possible. God said he had heard, had blessed Ishmael, would make him fruitful and greatly increase his numbers. He would be the father of twelve rulers and God would make him into a great nation. Nevertheless, Isaac was the son with whom God would establish his covenant (Genesis 17). If God changes our requests in this way we may be sure that there is some great purpose in it and that our prayer has been the source of the miracle to bring it about.

Lastly, you must observe the effects that denials have upon your spirit. Denials may cause you to acknowledge that God is holy and righteous in his dealings with you and that your own unworthiness is the cause of his denial. God may fill your heart with a holy contentment in the denial. When Paul prayed that the thorn in the flesh might be removed, God's answer was that his grace was sufficient for Paul. This made Paul content (2 Corinthians 12:9). You may still be thankful to God by trusting that whatever he has ordered for you is best, even though to your mind what has been denied would have been better. You are content with God's judgement in the matter. It is good if you can continue in prayer even when denied what you ask for. Fear the most when blessings are granted and love the most when they are denied! The Psalmist complained to God 'How long will your anger smoulder against the prayers of your people'? (Psalm 80:4). But he would not give up praying, even though God did not seem to hear. So you must pray on, even though you do not have an answer in this life. Even fair-minded people are moved by those who take rebuffs and denials well, for they know that proud people will not do this. God, also, is moved by such a humble attitude in his children.

10.

A reproof for those who will not look for blessings from their prayers.

Some people offer prayers and are earnest in begging things from God, but they do not pay any more regard to their prayers afterwards than if they had not prayed at all. They may have a great stock of prayers but they make no attempt to calculate what profits they have gained by praying. Instead, they become discouraged and doubt whether they will ever hear of their prayers again. They might as well have been speaking mere words into the air. Such people despise God's gracious provision for them, not knowing the power of prayer. They also despise the Lord himself. Not to answer when a question is put to you, is contempt; and not to take any notice when an answer is given is no less contemptuous. Suppose you had written a letter to a close friend about an important business and had urgently requested an answer. If you totally ignored his reply would you not be guilty of contempt? Or if you should not bother to read his answer when he wrote, would he not have cause to be angry with you? So here, when you have earnestly sought God over something and you take no notice of his answer you will be in contempt of God. This is a common fault among believers. You may not stop praying but you do not expect answers as you should. Let us look at the reasons for this.

1. The first is lack of assurance. Because you have a weak assurance that God accepts you as you are, your confidence that he will hear your prayers is also weak. God does first of all accept us as we are and this gives us confidence that he will also accept our prayers. As we saw in Chapter 1, this truth is found in 1 John 5:13-15, 'I write these things to you who believe in the name of the Son of God so that you may know that you have eternal life. This is the assurance we have in approaching God, that if we ask anything according to his will, he hears us. And if we know he hears us — whatever we ask — we know that we have what we asked of him'.

Notice how John links three things together as effects and consequences of each other. Firstly, he wants his readers to know that they may be assured that eternal life and heaven are theirs. Following from that will spring a confidence that God will hear them. God will have his ears open to them and his heart will be warm with love for them. Then thirdly, if they are confident that God hears them it will follow that they will have an assurance that God will grant them anything they desire that is according to his will. When we are assured that God has given us his Son we will then easily believe and expect that God will give us everything else that we need (Romans 8:32).

When we have grasped the fact that God is our Father we shall then easily understand the words of Jesus in Matthew 7:11, ' If you then, though you are evil, know how to give good gifts to your children, how much more will your Father in heaven give good gifts to those who ask him!' If God gave you his Son when you did not pray to him how much more will he give you the things you do pray for!

2. You may feel discouraged because your prayers are weak. You may believe that God accepts you as you are and yet complain that, because your prayers are poor and weak, God will not take any notice of them. We may answer this in four ways.

(a) Firstly, do you pray with all your might? Then even though that 'might' may be weak in itself, yet because it is all the might you have, it will be accepted. God accepts according to what we have, and not according to what we do not have (2 Corinthians 8:12).

(b) You must remember that God does not hear you for the sake of your prayers (though not without them), but for his name's sake, for his Son's sake, and because you are his child. When a child cries, the weaker it is the more a mother is concerned about it.

(c) Prayer may be weak as a performance yet it may still be strong enough. Even a weak prayer can set our strong God to work. Prayer succeeds, not because of the performance itself, but because of the name in which it is offered — even Christ's. Faith attributes all to God, and so does prayer. As faith is merely a *receiving* grace so prayer is a *begging* grace. God fully accepts even the weakest act of faith. Prayer is the means God has provided to convey his blessings, and so it does not matter whether it is weak or strong in our estimation of it.

(d) You must not judge your prayers by their eloquence or by the stirrings of heart you have when offering them. The strength and vigour of prayer is to be estimated from the faith, sincerity and obedience expressed in it. It is not the volume of the preacher's voice that moves an intelligent hearer, but the weight and holiness of the matter and the spirit of the preacher. It is not gifts, but graces, that move the Lord in prayer. The strength of prayer does not lie in words, but in the fact that it has the power to influence God. Prayers move God, not as an orator moves his hearers, but as a child moves his father. God is more concerned about the spirit in which we pray than in our choice of words.

3. A third discouragement is the failure to receive answers. You may have prayed often and long and yet your prayers have seldom or never been answered. You therefore have little

confidence that your prayers have ever been heard. Others have dividends from their prayers but you seem to get nothing. To deal with this problem note:

(a) You have the more reason to wait, for you may have the more answers to come. As wicked men treasure up wrath, so do godly men store up mercy, and especially by their prayers. Answers and blessings often come thick together.

(b) Even if you seem to have few answers, yet your reward is with the Lord. Praying is like preaching. A man may preach faithfully for many years and yet see no conversions. He must not give up but remind himself after every sermon that every worker will receive his reward according to his own labour (1 Corinthians 3:8). This reward does not depend on the success or otherwise of his preaching. When you pray, although you seem to miss again and again, you must not be discouraged because your reward is with the Lord and will be received one day.

(c) God may delay his answers, not because he does not hear you, but to test you. He may be testing your faithfulness in some duty.

(d) God may stay so long that you have given up expecting his answer. The elect cry day and night (Luke 18:7-8), but God stays so long that when he comes he does not find faith. His people have given up expecting and they have forgotten their prayers. It is then that God does things that they do not look for, for his own glory's sake.

4. There are other discouragements for which we ourselves are to blame. I will list three:

(a) Slothfulness in prayer. If we are not earnest and fervent in prayer, how can we expect God to give us anything good? Jacob obtained what he needed by praying (Genesis 32:24ff). Christ said that many will try to enter the kingdom of God, but you must make every effort to do so (Luke 13:24). When we know these things and yet are slothful, how can we expect any answers at all? God will behave as though he were asleep.

Those prayers that awaken God must first awaken us. Those prayers that stir God must first stir us to lay hold of God. As obedience strengthens faith and assurance, so fervency in prayer brings about the confidence of being heard. In all things, slothfulness discourages and weakens expectation. Does anyone expect that riches will come when he does his business negligently? You cannot expect an answer if you are slothful in prayer.

(b) Another cause of sinful discouragement is if you look at prayer only as a duty to be performed rather than as a means of obtaining blessings. Think of a doctor who has a sick employee and who prescribes a medicine for him, ordering him to take it. If the employee takes the medicine only as a matter of duty to please the doctor, but not in any way as a means of curing his illness, what sort of attitude is that? Most people seem to use prayer like that. They take prayer as a prescription only, but not as a means of blessing. They come to God daily, but only as to an employer by way of duty. They do not come to God as to a Father, and so it is small wonder if they have little expectation from their prayers. You should look for two things in prayer. Firstly, prayer is a command from God. Secondly, prayer is a means of receiving promised blessings. Prayer is firstly an act of obedience and secondly it is an act of faith in God's promises. When you ask you must 'believe and not doubt'. (James 1:6). Most people seem to perform prayer as an act of obedience only, but if you pray in faith, looking to God's promises, you may expect God to answer you.

(c) A third sinful discouragement is to return to sin after praying. If you have prayed for some blessing and are full of confidence that your prayers are heard, yet fall into sin, that sin will dash all your hopes. You will feel that you have wrecked your prayers and that they will not reach heaven. Sin may indeed hinder the obtaining of your petitions but it is not so much past sins that are a hindrance. It is more likely to be your present unhelpful attitude towards God which hinders your sense of blessing through prayer.